ANIMAL INVADERS

ANIMAL INVADERS

The Story of Imported Wildlife

Alvin and Virginia Silverstein

ATHENEUM 1974 NEW YORK

To Gil and Linda Wittlin

Copyright © 1974 by Alvin and Virginia Silverstein
All rights reserved
Library of Congress catalog card number 73–84835
ISBN 0–689–30146–4
Published simultaneously in Canada by
McClelland & Stewart, Ltd.
Manufactured in the United States of America
by Halliday Lithograph Corporation
West Hanover, Massachusetts
Designed by Nancy Gruber
First Edition

Contents

The Delicate Balance 3

A Success Story: The Ring-Necked Pheasant 13

Feathered Mistakes: Pigeons, Sparrows,
and Starlings 21

Strangers in the Streams: Muskrats and Nutrias 33

The Tale of the Mongoose 42

The Rabbit Plague 51

New Homes on the Range 64

The Case of the Walking Catfish and
Other Fish Stories 71

The Creeping Menace: The Giant African Snail 84

Insect Friends and Foes 92

The Future of Animal Transplants 113

Index 120

Caption credits 124

The Delicate Balance

In 1973, "Wanted" posters went up all over New Jersey for a new public enemy. He was about a foot tall, with a raucous chattering voice, and dressed in blue gray, green, and yellow feathers. He was commonly seen in forests and orchards, and his crime was destruction of fruits and other crops. His name was *Myiopsitta monachus,* alias the monk parakeet.

The monk parakeet is just one of the latest among the hordes of animal invaders who have left their native lands to find new homes. Some have slipped across the borders unseen, on their own or hitchhiking with unsuspecting humans. Some have been transplanted deliberately, for reasons that seemed very good at the time—yet the results have often been far from what people expected.

The monk parakeet's story is a typical one. For years, pet importers have been transporting monk parakeets from their homes in South America to bird lovers in the United States and various countries of Europe. This hardy bird makes a lively and intelligent pet, that can even be taught to talk with a little work and patience. But some people who have pets grow tired of them, and no longer wish to care for them. Then they are faced with a sad decision: what to do with a pet that is no longer welcome? Few people want to kill a pet that they have known and cared for, yet there may be no suitable person to whom it can be given. Often the kindest choice seems to be to release the animal in a nearby park or countryside—to give it a chance for a "free life."

Perhaps that was how the monk parakeet problem started in the United States. Or perhaps, as some bird experts believe, the monk parakeet invasion dates back to 1958, when a crate filled with the birds broke open at Kennedy Airport in New York, and they flew away.

However it began, the monk parakeets had found a new home. The climate was a little colder in New York than it was back in South America, but the birds did not seem to mind. They began to build their large nests of twigs, like bird apartment houses, on telephone poles and trees, and in the eaves of buildings. They laid their round white eggs, four, five or six at a time, and raised their young, and multiplied. Flocks of the chattering parakeets flew off to raid fields of corn or grains. They stole fruits from orchards, and between harvests they lived on seeds and berries of wild plants.

As the birds multiplied, they spread out, through New York and into neighboring New Jersey, and onward, toward Pennsylvania. Wildlife experts fear that if the monk parakeets are not stopped soon, they will some day

A new public enemy: the monk parakeet. (Above) a young bird; (below) an adult.

be found all through the country, from coast to coast. And wherever they live, they will be pests, eating farm crops and driving out more useful birds.

The people who brought monk parakeets to the United States should have been warned, for this bird was already a serious pest to food crops in its South American home. But even harmless-seeming animal invaders have proved to be unwelcome guests when they traveled to new lands and left their natural enemies behind. The tiny Chinese clams, for example, are called "good-luck clams" in South China, and they are considered a delicacy, a special treat to eat at New Year celebrations. No one is sure exactly how the little clams got to the United States, but they turned up in Oregon in 1938. Since then they have spread across the country, as far as the East coast. They do not seem to have any natural enemies here, and they develop much faster than American clams. So they just multiply and multiply. In California people found out just how fast the little Chinese clams can multiply when the Delta-Mendota Canal had to be drained for cleaning in 1969. The canal had been opened less than twenty years before. But there were beds of Chinese clams on the bottom more than 3 feet thick. (Each little clam is less than an inch long.) In some places there were as many as 5,000 clams in a single cubic foot. It took a month and a half of work with bulldozers to get the canal cleared out.

Scientists have some ideas about how the Chinese clams have spread across the country so quickly. Fishermen sometimes empty buckets of extra bait and thus may help to transfer clams to new rivers. Construction engineers dredge out bottom material from one river and may dump it into other rivers. Scientists think that ducks might even help to carry the tiny clams from place to place if they swallow them whole and the clams' hard shells protect their soft bodies inside the ducks' stomachs.

But how to stop the clams? That is something no one has figured out yet.

Like many animal invaders, Chinese clams became pests when they got to America by doing just what they did at home—only doing it a little better, because they had left their enemies behind. But some animal invaders have changed their habits in unexpected ways when they have found themselves in new surroundings.

What could be more harmless than a little gray squirrel? Scampering up and down the tree trunks, gathering nuts to hide for the long winter, chattering saucily, squirrels have always delighted people who watch them. Animal lovers are to be found all over the world. So it is not too surprising, perhaps, that the Duke of Bedford had ten of the American gray squirrels shipped to his English estate in 1890.

When the duke released his new squirrels, they cheerfully took to the trees and prospered. Soon there were plenty of extra squirrels on the estate, to be caught and given away to the duke's friends. Meanwhile, other Englishmen were sending for squirrels from America. Some were released in various parts of the British Isles. Others were kept as pets in cages. (But squirrels are rodents, with sharp gnawing teeth. Many pet squirrels chewed their way out of their cages and escaped to the freedom

Gray squirrels caused unexpected problems when they traveled to Britain.

of the woods.) By the time the last American squirrels were brought into Britain in 1910, the gray squirrel was already well established there. In fact, these squirrels were multiplying and spreading to new parts of the country each year.

Gray squirrels do not bother anyone in the United States. So what difference could it make that a few of them were transported to Britain? One effect that was soon noticed was that wherever gray squirrels invaded, the little native red squirrels began to disappear. No one is yet sure exactly why this happened. Perhaps the gray squirrels brought with them some squirrel disease against which their European cousins were defenseless. Perhaps, since the gray squirrels were larger and more aggressive than the red squirrels, they were simply better able to compete for food and living space. Perhaps, just by being there, in some strange way they made the red squirrels give up and not try hard enough to survive. Scientists have observed a very similar effect when large, aggressive Norway rats are placed in the same large cage with smaller black rats. Whatever the reason, the red squirrels continue to vanish from each new area that the gray squirrels occupy.

As if that were not bad enough, the gray squirrels that went to England suddenly began to behave in a very unsquirrellike fashion. Back home in America, they had been satisfied to eat seeds and nuts and tender green buds. From time to time they might invade a farmer's fields and eat his grain crops. But usually diseases, predators such as hawks and owls, times of drought or long hard winters, and other natural forces keep their numbers in check, and they have never been really serious pests. In fact, hunting laws in the United States usually protect gray squirrels at least for most of the year. But in England, gray squirrels suddenly began to eat the bark of trees. Sometimes they ate the bark completely around the trunks of young trees. A tree "girdled" in this way will die, for it must transport water and food materials through tiny tubes that run up the trunk in the living outer layer. In plantings of valuable hardwood trees, the gray squirrel quickly became a hated pest. The British government declared an open season on the American invaders, and even supplied hunters with free ammunition if they would use it to shoot squirrels. But the squirrels are still there, and they are still advancing each year.

The communities of nature—woodlands, meadows, deserts, ponds, rivers, oceans—are all in a delicate balance. Each has its own animals and plants. And some quite small areas have living things that are to be found nowhere else in the whole world. Yet each has its own place in its own community of life. Some are eaters, and some are the eaten. Even the eaters themselves are held in check by still other eaters, or diseases, or lack of enough food.

Man is constantly interfering with the balance of nature. Sometimes he does so unintentionally. He drains swamps or irrigates dry lands to grow his crops. He cuts roads through the wilderness and builds dams on rivers. Sometimes man changes natural communities on purpose, trying to improve them. He tries to kill all the predators, perhaps, or brings in some new creatures that he thinks would be just right for the area. Man has done so ever since he first began to move from place to place, long before there were written records of human history. But now, when animals and plants can be loaded onto an airplane and shipped halfway around the world in a matter of hours, it is easier than it ever has been for people to play at being gods and to try to shape the world to their own desires and whims.

When a new animal or plant is introduced into a delicately balanced natural community, or one of the old ones is taken away, there is a time of trouble. All the living things react to the change. Some find the new conditions favorable and do well—perhaps so well that they multiply faster than they ever have before. Others find themselves at a disadvantage, and they may dwindle away. Back and forth it goes, like a seesaw of feast and famine. At last a new balance is struck, and the living things of the community are in harmony once more. But often one or more kinds of animals or plants have disappeared forever, and the world is a little poorer for their loss.

For most of the world's history, people played at animal transplanting pretty much as they wished. But with the growing awareness of ecology, the science of how life forms are linked together, governments have begun to control plant and animal transplanters more and more. People who wish to bring wild animals from other countries into the United States now must first get the approval of the Bureau of Sport Fisheries and Wildlife, and the animals themselves must go through a period of quarantine to be sure they are not bringing any harmful diseases into the country. Some animals that might become dangerous pests—fruit bats, mongooses, certain mice and birds and catfishes, for example—may not be brought into the country at all. Other countries have similar regulations to guard their borders.

Yet even with all these rules and regulations, animal importing goes on. In 1969 alone, 116,341 mammals, 571,663 wild birds (not including canaries and parrots), 73,694,996 live fish, 1,938,533 mollusks and crustaceans, 339,489 frogs and other amphibians, and 1,393,970 reptiles entered the United States. May of these were brought in by private importers to sell as pets. But even government agencies continue to bring in foreign wild animals to try to establish new kinds of game animals, to cope with native and imported pests, and for various other reasons. It seems certain that this game of international "animal musical chairs" will continue to go on. And thus it might be wise to look at some of the lessons of the past. Perhaps they might help us to avoid making similar mistakes in the future.

A Success Story:
The Ring-Necked Pheasant

The dream of people who bring in exotic animals from foreign lands is to find an animal that adapts readily to the conditions of its new home, thrives and multiplies, fills a need such as food or recreation, does not interfere with native wildlife species, and does not become an agricultural pest or disease carrier. So far, the animal immigrant to the United States that has come closest to being a dream come true is the ring-necked pheasant.

Pheasants belong to a family of birds that includes the quails, partridges, and chickens. Like their relatives, they normally spend most of their time on the ground but can take to flight for short distances if they are frightened. But unlike chickens, pheasants have never been completely domesticated. Even after generations of being raised in cages, pheasants quickly go wild if they are let free. This trait makes it easy to restock the wild populations of pheasants in areas where hunting or predators have reduced their numbers.

The male pheasant is a handsome bird, with brightly colored, iridescent feathers and a long, pointed tail. Ring-necked pheasants (*Phasianus colchicus*), get their name from a ring of white feathers around the neck of the male. He is about 3 feet long, has a dark green head with a pair of feather "ears," a chickenlike body and wings covered with multicolored feathers, a long straight tail, and a pair of fighting spurs on the back of his legs.

The female ring-necked pheasant is drab in comparison. But her dull-brown, mottled feathers serve her well as camouflage when she is sitting on her eggs in a small hollow that she has scratched out in the ground.

Ring-necked pheasants are normally found in and around farmlands. They prefer to live in open woodlands and meadows with trees, for they roost in trees at night. But they come out into open fields for feeding. In country areas they can often be seen walking along by the side of the road. The male pheasant's feeding territory is criss-crossed by a system of paths, which he patrols regularly, stopping every now and then to flap his wings and crow.

Pheasants scratch the ground for food as chickens do, with their strong, clawed toes. They eat seeds and berries, insects, fallen leaves and fruit, and any roots, bulbs, and tubers they happen to scratch up. They also eat worms, slugs, and snails, small lizards and snakes, and even mice and other small rodents. Unless they become so numerous that they begin raiding crops, pheasants are generally a help to the farmer because they eat insects and other pests.

Pheasants themselves make good eating, and they have

A handsome male ring-necked pheasant struts through a corn-field with his inconspicuous mate.

been prized by hunters as game birds for many centuries. When a pheasant is flushed by a bird dog, he may fly almost straight up, before dropping quickly into cover again. Though he cannot fly long distances, his flight is extremely fast—it is claimed he can go up to 60 miles an hour.

In the spring, the male ring-necked pheasant takes a mate—or two or more if there are enough pheasants living in the area. In April, when it is time for mating, the cock parades before the hen pheasant, displaying his fine feathered coat. He droops the wing closest to her and curves his tail toward her, so that she can see his full array to best advantage. His wattles, which can barely be seen in the winter, are swollen and fiery red during the mating season.

After mating, the hen pheasant scratches out a hollow for a nest in some sheltered place and lines it with leaves and grass. She lays from eight to fifteen olive-brown eggs and sits on them for the twenty-three days it takes them to hatch.

If a fox or some other predator comes near while a mother pheasant is sitting on her nest, or later when there are chicks in the nest, she will try to lead the predator away. She jumps up and rushes off, dragging one wing as though she is injured. While her chicks slip quietly out of the nest into the underbrush and crouch there, motionless, the predator follows the hen pheasant. When she has led him far enough away, she takes to her wings and flies in a wide arc back to the nest.

The downy pheasant chicks quickly get their adult feathers, and after two weeks they can already fly well. The mother and her brood remain in the cock's territory until the young are about half-grown.

There is an ancient Greek legend that when Jason and his Argonauts sailed off to Colchis (in what is now the USSR) to capture the Golden Fleece, they brought back pheasants with them. There may be some truth to the legend, for the ancient Greeks did found a colony in Colchis, called Phasis, and the name of the pheasants comes from a Greek word meaning "native of Phasis." Before long, pheasant raising was a common practice in Greece.

When the Romans conquered the Greeks, they took over many Greek customs, and pheasant raising was one of them. Pheasants were one of the delicacies served at rich Roman banquets.

The Romans helped to spread pheasants to other countries of Europe, and this spread continued after the fall of the Roman Empire. By the sixteenth century, pheasant hunting was so popular in England and Germany that laws had to be made to protect the game pheasants.

By the time America was settled, and immigrants from England had begun to dream longingly of the pheasant hunting back home, the pheasant already had a long record of travels and transplantations. Ring-necked pheasants, originally found in Eastern Europe and Asia, from the Caucasus in Russia eastward to China and Formosa, now could be found in most of Europe. There were a number of varieties of ring-necked pheasants—some of them lacked the white ring around the neck of the cock—and there was much cross-breeding among them.

The first attempts to establish ring-necked pheasants in the United States occurred long before the colonies won their independence. In 1730, the governor of New York released half-a-dozen pairs of pheasants. But they soon disappeared. Benjamin Franklin's son-in-law, Richard Bache, tried to establish pheasants on his estate in New Jersey. But the birds he imported suffered a similar fate. The pheasants sent to George Washington as a gift by the Marquis de Lafayette in 1786 also failed to thrive in the new land.

Through the years the attempts went on, but still the ring-necked pheasant could not be successfully transplanted from Europe to the United States. Then, in 1877,

Judge Owen Denny was appointed a U.S. consul in Shanghai, China. In his new post, Judge Denny quickly gained an appreciation for Chinese cooking, particularly the delicious roast pheasant. He decided to send some of the Chinese pheasants back to his home in the Willamette Valley in Oregon, so that he would be able to enjoy his new favorite dish when he returned. In 1881 he bought about sixty ring-necked pheasants, together with some partridges and sand grouse, packed them in wicker basket cages, and shipped them back to a friend in Oregon, with instructions to turn them loose in various parts of the state. Unfortunately, the trip across the ocean was a rough one, and the birds arrived battered and ill. Though Judge Denny's friend released them, all the birds soon disappeared.

Judge Denny was disappointed, but he did not give up. A year later he had a large, roomy bamboo cage built securely into the hold of the ship *Isle of Bute*. The floor of the 20-foot-square cage was covered with gravel, and tubs of native shrubbery were brought in to make the birds feel at home. Then ten cock pheasants and eighteen hens were placed in the cage.

When the *Isle of Bute* docked in Portland, Oregon, after its voyage across the ocean, Judge Denny's pheasants were in fine shape. As he had requested, his brother met the boat this time and released the birds behind the Denny home. The pheasants found their new home ideal, and they settled down to the serious business of nesting.

By the time Judge Denny and his wife returned to Portland in 1884, people in neighboring counties were already spotting "Denny's pheasants" strutting along the roads. In 1891, the state of Oregon declared the first open season on pheasants—and 50,000 of the birds were taken!

Other states heard of the ring-necked pheasant's success in Oregon and clamored for pheasants of their own. Some of the Oregon pheasants were live-trapped and shipped to other states. In 1911, the state began a large-scale program of incubating pheasant eggs. Eventually forty-eight states tried to establish pheasants on their lands. Some were enormously successful. Ring-necked pheasants prospered so well in South Dakota that hunters flock in from all over the country for the pheasant hunting season. In 1943, the ring-necked pheasant was named the official state bird by the South Dakota state legislature.

It was estimated that South Dakota spent about $20,000 and released about 7,000 birds to introduce the ring-necked pheasant. But many states spent far more money and put in much more effort, with far less success. In all, the ring-necked pheasant has been established in only nineteen states.

Why have some states been so much more successful than others in introducing the ring-necked pheasant? It seems that, although this pheasant is a hardy and adaptable bird, a number of things limit its distribution. So far the ring-necked pheasant has been successful only in northern and western states. Scientists looking at a map realized that the southern limits of its distribution agrees almost exactly with the end of the glaciers' advance in the last Ice Age. Perhaps, they thought, the birds might need a certain amount of calcium in their food, in order for their eggs to hatch properly. And food grown in soil from areas over which glaciers once passed is richer in calcium than food from areas that the glaciers never reached. Some laboratory experiments were tried, and sure enough —calcium is one of the factors that limits where the ring-necked pheasant can survive. Another limiting factor is climate. Hot, humid weather, which is typical of the southern states, cuts down the hatching of ring-necked pheasant eggs. The use of mowing machines, which disturb the hen pheasants on their nests and kill many young, is probably another part of the picture.

The ring-necked pheasant now found in the United States is a crossbreed of at least four or five different varieties of *Phasianus colchicus*. Indeed, it is rare to find two ring-necked cocks with exactly the same colors, and some even lack the white "collar." Many more varieties of the game pheasant are still to be found in Asia. Researchers are now experimenting with new varieties and crossbreeds of pheasants, trying to find some that will permit the southern states to share in the success story of the ring-necked pheasant.

Ring-neck pheasant chicks are hatching.

Feathered Mistakes: Pigeons, Sparrows, and Starlings

Pigeons, sparrows, and starlings are probably more familiar to city dwellers in the United States than any other kind of birds. Yet not one of these birds lived in America before the first European settlers came to the continent.

The pigeon (*Columba livia*) was the first to arrive, carried by some of the early settlers. In a way that is quite fitting, for pigeons have been associated with man for at least five thousand years. Their ancestors, the plump-bodied rock doves of Europe and Asia, may have been the first birds to be domesticated. They have been prized ever since as sources of delicious, easily digested meat.

Pigeons have an amazing homing sense. If a pigeon is carried away from its home, even in a covered cage so that it cannot see where it is going, it will fly straight home as soon as it is released. It can steer a course by the positions of the sun and stars in the sky. An amazing inner clock adjusts for changes according to the time of day. The ancient Greeks took advantage of the pigeons' homing instinct by using these birds as messengers, more than four hundred years before Christ. Carrier pigeons brought the news to Rome that Caesar had conquered Gaul, and, centuries later, a homing pigeon brought the news of Napoleon's defeat at Waterloo to Paris. Even today, carrier pigeons have their uses. A modern hospital worked out a system by which doctors out on house calls could strap test tubes of blood or other body fluids of a patient to a pigeon. The bird could deliver the specimens to the hospital for tests far faster than an automobile could carry them through crowded city streets.

Domestic pigeons sometimes escape from their cages and sometimes are turned loose by owners who no longer want to care for them. These pigeons quickly go wild and adapt easily to living on their own. Within a few generations, the gaudy feathers of show pigeons, carefully bred by men over many centuries, are gone—the descendants of tame pigeons gone wild have the same bluish-gray feathered coats as their wild ancestors, the rock doves. But most of the pigeons gone wild do not go out to the countryside to nest in caves and feed on seeds, snails, insects, and worms, as the rock doves do. Instead they stay in the city, where the living is easy. Huge flocks of pigeons live in most of the large cities of the world, roosting on statues and in sheltered nooks on buildings, eating the food that pigeon lovers conveniently put out for them, and filling the air with their peaceful-sounding cooing.

Pigeon populations grow quickly. The female pigeon builds a flimsy platform of twigs and straw and other materials that the male brings her and lays one or two white eggs. Both parents take turns sitting on the eggs, the male during the day and the female at night. In two-and-a-half weeks the eggs hatch, and then both parents feed the helpless young. For the first ten days the chicks eat a special "pigeon milk," which is made in the adult pigeon's crop. The babies eat this food right out of their parents' throats. Gradually seeds and fruits are substituted, and after a few weeks the young are ready to leave the nest. The parents care for them a while longer, but meanwhile they have very likely started a new brood of eggs.

The wild pigeon populations of cities have always been rather a nuisance, soiling statues and buildings with their droppings. (Pigeon droppings make good fertilizer, but

Flocks of pigeons are a common sight in most cities.

they are an expensive cleaning problem for.the cities.) But in the past few decades, medical scientists have begun to realize that pigeons can be responsible for a far more serious problem: they carry diseases, some of which can be transmitted to humans.

City life offers an easy life and protection from the hawks and other birds of prey that are the main enemies of pigeons in the countryside. But the bread that people generally feed them does not provide a very well-balanced diet. For one thing, it does not contain enough calcium, and the pigeons must often peck at the mortar of buildings to get enough of this important mineral to make shells for their eggs. (Needless to say, this practice does not do the buildings any good.) The poor diet and the crowded conditions make city pigeons easy prey to disease and parasites. In one study in Chicago, it was found that 45 percent of the city's pigeons were carrying the virus of ornithosis, or parrot fever. This is a serious disease, which in humans has symptoms like those of viral pneumonia. Pigeon droppings also spread fungus diseases such as histoplasmosis (a serious lung disease) and a form of meningitis, and the parasite responsible for toxoplasmosis, a disease that can cause blindness and serious birth defects in unborn children if it is caught during pregnancy. Tiny particles of dried pigeon droppings drift through the air and are inhaled by the city dweller with every breath. Mosquitoes that bite infected pigeons can spread a virus that causes encephalitis, a serious disease of the brain. Bird mites, bedbugs, and ticks are parasites that pigeons can spread to humans.

Feeding pigeons may be fun, but it can cause serious problems.

When scientists began to realize how dangerous pigeons can be, many cities passed laws making it illegal to feed pigeons. Then they set about searching for ways to get rid of their pigeon populations. One approach was to poison or shoot the pigeons. But this approach usually met with cries of outrage from pigeon lovers. Many people enjoy feeding pigeons and refuse to believe there can be any harm in it.

The city of Paris tried to cope with its pigeon problem by catching the pigeons in a huge net, baited with food. The pigeons that were caught were carefully transported to a village more than a hundred miles away, fed for a few days, then released. Of course, this did not work at all. The pigeons promptly used their homing sense and flew right back to Paris.

Various other ideas are being tried, such as stringing electrified wires on buildings where unwanted pigeons are in the habit of roosting. Perhaps the most promising approach is one that scientists are working on now: adding birth control chemicals to the pigeons' food, to prevent them from adding new generations to the cities' flocks.

English sparrows did not come to America with the earliest settlers. Indeed, the first successful introduction of these birds was not made until 1853, when about fifty of them were turned loose in Greenwood Cemetery in Brooklyn, New York. But the sparrows soon made up for their late start. These hardy little birds have lived with man for thousands of years and can even thrive in industrialized cities, where few other birds can survive. They fly about in noisy flocks and feed mainly on grains, but also on weed seeds, buds, fruits, caterpillars, and insects such as Japanese beetles. America of the nineteenth century was a paradise for English sparrows—all they had to do for a ready food supply was to follow the horses that clattered up and down the streets. Tasty sparrow food was to be found not only in the horses' feed bags, but also in the undigested parts of their droppings.

The English sparrow is also called the house sparrow (*Passer domesticus*), because of its habit of living among men's dwellings. Sparrows build a loosely woven nest of straw, rags, and string inside some sheltered place, such as a birdhouse, a woodpecker's hole, or a drain spout. The female sparrow lays five or six spotted white eggs, which hatch in less than two weeks. The young birds grow quickly, yet their mother may have laid a new clutch of eggs before they have even left the nest. She and her mate may raise four broods in a year.

While the first sparrows in Brooklyn were busily multiplying and spreading out to new territories, American sparrow lovers were enthusiastically helping the cause. Englishmen and Germans were astonished to be showered with money for house sparrows that they were delighted to get rid of. To them, sparrows were pests. These aggressive little birds often chase away songbirds from nesting and feeding places. When they leave the cities for the

English sparrows, another feathered mistake. The bird (left) is a female; the bird (right) a male.

countryside, they become more than a nuisance. Though they eat their share of harmful insects, their flocks can quickly strip a grain crop in a field and beat down the stems, and they boldly steal the feed of chickens and other farm animals.

But in America the sparrow craze went on. Sparrows were released in cities from Maine to California, from Quebec in Canada down to Texas. As soon as the sparrows became well established in one locality, sparrow fanciers took pairs of them to other parts of the country.

The sparrows prospered—and gradually people began to wonder whether it had been such a good idea to bring them over after all. Farmers were complaining about the damage flocks of raiding sparrows were doing to their crops. Sparrow droppings were killing the ornamental plants around city buildings. People in cities and towns were beginning to miss the native songbirds that seemed to have disappeared after the sparrows had come. The house sparrows' monotonous chirping hardly seemed an even exchange. Laws protecting the sparrows were repealed, and soon the same communities that had encouraged the birds were offering bounties for them.

It was too late—the sparrows were already too well established, and efforts to get rid of them hardly dented their population. The invention of the motorcar did cut down the numbers of house sparrows in cities somewhat, by eliminating their easiest source of food. But these hardy little invaders are here to stay.

People should have learned a lesson from the transplanting of the sparrow, and perhaps they did to some degree. At least no one takes sparrows to new homes any-more. (That is small consolation, since house sparrows are already well established in North and South America, South Africa, Australia, and New Zealand, as well as parts of Asia and their original homes in Europe!) But though Americans were hurriedly trying to think of ways to get rid of the sparrows they had recently brought in, it seemed not to occur to anyone that the same problems might be encountered in starlings.

The common starling (*Sturnus vulgaris*) is a handsome bird. For much of the year, his feathers are a glossy black, iridescent with flashes of purple, green, and blue. In the winter, his coat becomes spangled with white. Starlings are noisy birds, constantly calling loudly to the others in the flock. They are good mimics, and can imitate not only the calls of other birds, but even the sounds of machines and other noises. A group of workmen who were cutting down trees with a power saw once had a startling demon-stration of the starling's mimicking ability. While they were eating lunch, a starling serenaded them with a per-fect imitation of the sound of a power saw and the crash-ing of a falling tree, complete with rustling leaves and swishing branches.

The starling's ability as a mimic was the indirect cause of the bird's being brought to America. There is a line in Shakespeare's play, *Henry IV,* "Nay, I'll have a starling shall be taught to speak nothing but 'Mortimer.' " In the late 1800s, a New York drug manufacturer, Eugene Schieffelin, had an ingenious idea. Since he was both a bird lover and a Shakespeare fan, he decided to bring

A flock of starlings comes in to roost near Danbury, Connecticut.

Starlings settle in for the night.

to America all the birds that the great bard had mentioned. In 1890 he had sixty starlings released in Central Park in New York City. This was not the first attempt to introduce starlings to America, but it was the first successful one. That same year, Schieffelin's starlings began nesting. (Appropriately, the first nest was found across from the park, under the eaves of The American Museum of Natural History.) Clutches of eggs—four to nine pale blue eggs at a time—were hatched, and the young were raised and went on to mate and raise young of their own. Another group of starlings introduced in 1891 added to the flock. Starlings spread through the boroughs of New York and out into the suburbs. Years went by. Starlings were spotted in Canada and in Georgia. The starlings moved westward to the Mississippi, onward past the Great Plains, over the Rocky Mountains and on to the west coast. From the original flock in Central Park, the starlings have now spread to all the states of the Union. They mingle with other blackbirds in flocks that often number in the millions.

In the 1920s a panel was set up to study the effects of starlings on agriculture in the United States. In some ways, starlings are helpful to the farmer. They probe the ground with their sharp beaks for insects and grubs and are an important check on wireworms and Japanese beetles. During the summer, as much as 90 percent of their food may be animal matter of this kind. But in other seasons of the year they feed on fruits and berries. They raid beef and hog feedlots, stealing much of the grain and often fouling the rest with their droppings. They drive out other hole-nesting birds such as bluebirds and flickers. Annoying as they are in the countryside, starlings are even more of a pest in the city. They roost on buildings, fouling them with their droppings and keeping people awake with their constant cries. Starling droppings, like pigeon droppings, have been shown to carry diseases. Flocks of starlings have even caused airplane crashes, when the birds were swept into the engines and caused them to flame out.

People have fought back against starlings in a variety of ways. Shotgun blasts, traps, electrified window ledges, a sticky substance called "Roost No More," and fire-crackers and stuffed owls to frighten the birds have all been tried. In one novel approach, scientists at Pennsylvania State University studied starling calls and identified their special distress cry. They recorded this cry and then played back the recording through a loudspeaker. The starlings left—though not always for good.

Scientists continue their research for a way to decrease the starlings, but at the moment, at least, it seems that starlings, like sparrows, are a permanent part of our wildlife.

Strangers in the Streams: Muskrats and Nutrias

People living in cold climates have always envied animals their lovely warm fur coats, and they have caught animals for their furs since before the Stone Age. The first business started in the New World, in 1670, was the Hudson's Bay Company.

Today artificial furs have been developed, which are as soft and warm as real furs and can be dyed in any color of the rainbow. Many people are worried that some of the world's most beautiful animals may become extinct, and have urged that artificial fur coats be bought instead of real ones. But other people still prefer real furs, and in 1972 fur sales in the United States alone amounted to $355 million. Many of the animals most often used for furs are in no danger of disappearing from the earth. Mink and chinchillas are raised by the millions on ranches. Millions of wild muskrats, raccoons, and nutrias are trapped each year, and there are no signs that their numbers are decreasing. In fact, in some places there are entirely too many muskrats and nutrias to please anybody. Neither muskrats nor nutrias cause any trouble in their original homes. It is just when people have taken them to new homes that they have brought some unpleasant surprises.

Muskrats (*Ondatra zibethica*) are found in most of North America. They live in marshes, ponds, and sluggish streams, and they look like little beavers. About the size of a rabbit, a muskrat has thick, soft, shiny fur that helps to protect him from chills when he swims in the water. His long, flattened tail and hairy-toed, partly webbed hind feet help him to paddle along. He gets his name from a pair of musk glands at the base of his tail. The muskrat leaves his scent at landing places along the shore, to tell other muskrats he has been there.

Like his cousin the beaver, the muskrat may build a dome-shaped house in the middle of a pond or stream, rising a few feet above the surface of the water. He builds with cattails and mud and leaves a hollowed out sleeping chamber inside, which he lines with a thick bed of dry leaves. If the stream where he lives and works has a soft, muddy bank, the muskrat will hollow out a burrow there instead, with an entrance underwater. Channels branch out through the swamp from the muskrat's den. He generally patrols these channels early in the morning and at evening, snipping off cattails and various other water plants with his sharp, chisellike front teeth, digging up roots, nibbling at bark and berries, and occasionally making a meal of frogs or mussels, or even fish. Usually the muskrat takes his food to some sheltered spot to eat— under an overhanging bank, or inside an eating hut of cattails. His best defense against enemies such as mink, weasels, hawks, and owls is to stay out of sight as much as possible.

It seemed a sensible idea to raise muskrats on "fur farms," like mink and chinchillas. Muskrats are rapid breeders. A female muskrat gives birth to between four and nine tiny, blind, naked young, less than a month after she has mated. The babies grow quickly. After a month, their mother weans them and drives them out of the nest, for she has mated again and will soon give birth to another litter. She can have three or more litters each year.

Unfortunately for would-be muskrat farmers, muskrats like to have plenty of room. When their home territories grow crowded, fights break out, mothers abandon their young, and the animals become easy prey to disease and

Muskrat houses in Minnesota.

predators. In muskrat farms, just as the population is building up to the kind of figures the muskrat raiser is pleased with, many of the young muskrats tunnel under the fences and leave in search of more living space.

Ondatra zibethica was originally found only in the New World. The Old World had its own little water rat, a small animal with long fluffy fur, which lives quietly in the banks of rivers and ponds and does not bother anybody. But many people thought that New World muskrats would be a valuable addition to European ponds and streams. So in 1905, Prince Colleredo-Mannsfeld of Czechoslovakia ordered some muskrats from Alaska and released two males and three females near Prague. Later more muskrats were brought in from Canada.

Over the next few years, the muskrats began to spread out, annexing 30 to 45 square miles of new territory each year. Muskrats invaded Germany, Romania, Yugoslavia, Austria, Poland, and Russia. In the swamps of Russia, and then in Finland, the muskrats became a valuable new fur animal.

Around 1927, some enterprising Frenchmen brought muskrats into their country to raise on fur farms. But like the Americans, they quickly found that the furry rodents did not do well on crowded fur farms. Soon muskrats were loose and spreading through the French countryside. Meanwhile, descendants of the original muskrats from Czechoslovakia were moving from Germany into Belgium and Holland.

Muskrats were taken to Britain, too. In 1927, 5 females and 4 males escaped from a fur farm in Scotland.

In the next three years, nearly 900 of their descendants were trapped.

In America, muskrats are not a problem, but a valuable natural resource. In addition to their fine fur, they help to keep the waterways open by eating waterweeds. But in many parts of Europe, the muskrat's habits bring disaster. In Holland and in other European countries, dikes hold back the sea and keep it from flooding over the flat land. Muskrats dig into the earthen dikes, causing leaks that can crumble them. The creatures also dig into the walls of drainage and irrigation ditches, flooding some fields and draining others. They tunnel into railroad embankments, and undermine bridges. In drier areas they make pests of themselves by eating farmers' crops.

The first attempt to halt the muskrats' advance was a

The muskrat—no problem in its native home.

massive trapping program in Bavaria in 1917. But still the muskrats spread. England was luckier. In an expensive five-year effort, starting in 1932, the British managed to wipe out all of the muskrats that had spread through the British Isles. Strict laws forbidding the transportation and keeping of muskrats may keep Britain free of what are for them water pests.

In other European countries, muskrats are still a problem. Germany and Holland employ official trappers to catch these imported rodents. Holland faces an even more serious threat. In addition to government-paid trappers, the Dutch have a bounty system that netted 21,000 muskrats in 1971 alone. But these were not all Dutch muskrats. When the bounties were begun, a brisk trade in smuggled muskrats quickly sprang up. Belgian trappers sold their muskrat catches to Dutchmen, who made a tidy profit by turning the rodents in for the bounty.

While muskrats gone wild still plague the countries of Europe, back in America the muskrat himself has a new and troublesome neighbor: the coypu, or nutria of South America.

The nutria (*Myocastor coypu*) looks rather like an overgrown muskrat. Its reddish-brown, soft, thick underfur is covered by a coat of long, coarse guard hairs. (When nutria fur is sold, the guard hairs are plucked out, and only the underfur is used.) Its hind feet are webbed, and it has a scaly, ratlike tail.

During the nineteenth century, nutrias were hunted so intensively in their South American homes that they nearly disappeared. Laws had to be passed to protect them. Shipments of nutrias were sent to countries in various parts of the world to be raised in pens on fur farms. But like the muskrats, the nutrias quickly escaped from the fur farms. Soon wild populations were established in North America, England, various countries of the European continent, and the USSR.

The runaway nutrias multiplied rapidly. The male nutria lives with a harem of two or three females. Each of his mates has two litters of young a year, with up to nine babies in each. A young nutria develops inside its mother's body much longer than a muskrat does—more than four months. By the time it is born, its eyes are open, and it has a full coat of fur. Within hours it is moving about actively; before it is one day old, it is venturing out of the family burrow and swimming after its mother in the swamp.

The nutria mother is unusually well adapted for family life in the water. Nearly all female mammals have their nipples on the belly. But the mother nutria's nipples are so high on her flanks that they are nearly on her back. They are above the waterline when she swims, and thus her little ones can drink her milk as they travel. Often they ride along on her back. They are weaned at two months and can mate a month later, before they are fully grown.

In England, the first wild nutrias were discovered in the 1930s, shortly after the first nutria farms were set up. Then, as the war began, the nutria farms were closed down, and the animals were usually released into the local waterways. At first the South American invaders were

The nutria brought more trouble than its fur coat was worth.

regarded as a welcome addition to British wildlife. Their burrows did not undermine the riverbanks, and they helped to keep the waterways clear. But as the hungry nutrias multiplied, they began to raid crops. There were reports of lines of nutrias, chomping their way across sugar beet fields in the moonlight, or leveling wheat fields to feed on the grains. A campaign was begun to get rid of the nutrias, and although not all of them have been killed, they have been driven back to an area around Norfolk.

The first attempt to get nutrias started in the United States was made in California in 1899, but the nutrias died out. Then, in 1938, a Louisiana industrialist, E. A. McIlhenny, brought in six pairs from Argentina. These nutrias did well in the Louisiana marsh, and were kept well penned in until 1940, when a hurricane flooded the marshes. About 150 nutrias swam over the flooded fences and took to the bayous and lakes. By 1956, it was estimated that nutrias were living wild in at least eighteen southern states.

The spread of the nutria in the United States was helped by a wild advertising campaign. Unscrupulous nutria promoters raved about the high profits that could be made from these amazing new fur animals, and people paid up to a thousand dollars for a breeding pair. By the time the Better Business Bureau launched an investigation and found that these fantastic claims were false, there were disillusioned nutria raisers all over the country. Many of them turned their nutrias free in disgust, even though some states, such as Oregon, had laws against it.

As the value of nutria pelts dropped to less than a dollar each, the nutrias were proving to be real pests. Although they did not interfere with the more valuable muskrats, whose habitat they shared, they began to feed in flooded rice fields, as well as in fields of corn, lettuce, and other crops. Their digging undermined the levees used in flooding the rice fields, and the broken levees often caused the fields to wash out suddenly.

The United States Fish and Wildlife Service established a nutria research station in Louisiana to search for ways to control nutria damage. After a while the demand for nutria fur increased, and nutria trapping became profitable once more. So this South American rodent still paddles contentedly through the waterways of the world.

The Tale of the Mongoose

Today, more and more, people are worried about pollution. Industry, homes, and cars send soot and chemicals into the air, sometimes producing poisonous smog. Solid wastes of our throw-away society litter the countryside. Chemical pesticides are washed from the fields by the rains into rivers and streams and find their way into our foods and even our own bodies. Sometimes pesticides kill the fish in streams and lakes. DDT in the bodies of eagles and hawks makes them lay eggs with shells so thin that they break before they can hatch.

Yet with nearly 4 billion people in the world to feed, we cannot just let pests run wild, to eat and spoil our crops. So people are searching for better ways to control harmful insects, rodents, and other pests. One of the suggestions has been to use biological means of pest control —to find and introduce natural enemies and diseases that will kill the pests but leave other animals unharmed. This seems like a particularly logical answer to the problem when it is a question of imported pests, which have been brought into new lands either accidentally or on purpose, and then have run wild. Scientists point out, quite rightly, that one of the main reasons such animal invaders do so much better in their new home than anyone ever expected is that they have left their natural enemies behind. So what better solution could there be than to bring in the pests' natural enemies and let nature take care of its own?

Many people act as though biological pest control were a brand new idea that holds foolproof solutions to every problem. Indeed, biological solutions are probably the best ones for many problem pests, but the approach is not new at all. The taming of the cat was an early attempt to get rid of pesky rats and mice—and that happened long before man had even learned to write. And natural predators and diseases for runaway pests can sometimes develop into problems themselves, in ways that no one ever expected. The stories of past mistakes hold lessons that we should heed today.

Christopher Columbus discovered the island of Jamaica in 1494, on his second voyage to the New World. It was a green island paradise, with a balmy climate and a lush growth of forests. Gradually settlers came from Europe, bringing with them some new crop plants, such as breadfruit and sugarcane. Soon cane sugar was an important crop on the island, grown on large plantations. But the settlers had brought some animal invaders along with them, although they did not realize it at first. Black rats and Norway rats had stowed away on the ships, and some of them settled in Jamaica, too. The thickly growing

The Norway rat, one of the champion world travelers. This mother rat built a nest for her litter in the corner of a storeroom.

sugarcane stalks provided both shelter and an easy source of food for the rat immigrants, and they prospered and multiplied. Native rats on the island also found the cane fields an unexpected rodent paradise, and they had their own population explosion.

Soon plantation owners were complaining about the crop losses caused by those pesky rats. It was hard to catch and kill the pests, because the cane fields provided so many good places for a rat to hide. Farmers even tried burning off the fields, but the rats were as numerous as ever.

In 1762, Thomas Raffle, one of the planters, got an idea. He knew of a big, vicious ant that lived in Cuba. This ant (*Formica omnivora*) was said to be so ferocious that it bit birds and small mammals to death. It should be just the thing to get rid of the rats in the cane fields. So Thomas Raffle sent to Cuba for a shipment of the big ants and turned them loose in his fields.

At first it seemed that the ants were just what the planters had been hoping for. They did indeed kill many young rats, and they multiplied and spread over the island. But then, for some reason, the rats began multiplying again. And the "Tom Raffle ants," as the Jamaicans now called them, soon became pests in their own right. They did not bite just rats, they bit young birds and anything else that came their way.

Another plantation owner, Anthony Davis, got a new idea. There was a big toad called *Bufo marinus,* which swept up insects like a vacuum cleaner. All Jamaica needed was a stock of these toads, and the ant problem

Bufo marinus, *the toad that brought more problems to Jamaica than it solved.*

would soon be over. In fact, *Bufo marinus* was so big and fast that he could probably take care of the young rats, too.

Anthony Davis brought in a shipment of the giant toads, and the toads did indeed begin devouring young rats, Tom Raffle ants, and various other insect pests for good measure. But the numbers of the pests did not shrink fast enough to suit the plantation owners. Besides, dog owners were soon complaining. The toads were equipped with poison glands, and if a dog bit one of them, he would die. So people began looking around for something that would kill off the rats faster—and perhaps the toads, if they got out of hand.

European ferrets, bloodthirsty little weasels, which had long been trained as rat and rabbit catchers, were tried. But the chiggers that live in Jamaica bothered the ferrets so much that they never really prospered and gradually disappeared.

Then, in 1872, a sugarcane raiser named W. B. Espeut had nine mongooses shipped from India, four males and five females. He turned them loose in his fields and waited to see what would happen.

The stories of Rudyard Kipling have made the Indian mongoose famous as a cobra killer. There are actually a number of kinds of mongooses; the one that was sent to Jamaica is called by scientists *Herpestes javanicus*. The mongoose is not a very large animal. Its body is about a foot long, and it has nearly another foot of long, furry tail. It weighs just about a pound when it is full grown.

Mongooses can be tamed, and they make charming and

intelligent pets. But a mongoose in the wilds is a deadly killer. It goes after a variety of reptiles, amphibians, birds, rodents, and insects. It uses its lightning-fast reflexes to help it kill snakes, even the deadly cobra. When a mongoose meets a snake, it waits for the snake to strike. Then it quickly steps aside and pounces on the snake's head, crushing the skull with a single bite of its powerful jaws.

There are two things about the mongoose that would have made today's ecology-minded scientists pause before bringing it in for a job of rat killing. First of all, mongooses are active during the daytime, retiring to a burrow or a hollow tree to sleep at night; and rats are nocturnal animals, active mainly after the sun has set. Secondly, in their native home mongooses do indeed eat rats, but they also eat snakes, lizards, frogs, crabs, eggs, and a variety of other things, sometimes including leaves and fruit. They eat mainly whatever is around in the greatest supply.

But Mr. Espeut was not an ecologist. He was just a sugarcane planter who was tired of losing a large fraction of his crop to the rats each year. He had to try *something*!

At first Mr. Espeut was delighted with his mongooses. They started right in on the job of rat killing, and soon the losses of sugarcane on his plantation were lower than anywhere else on the island. Other plantation owners begged him for some of his mongooses, but Mr. Espeut refused to part with a single one. So fieldworkers slipped into his fields at night, trapped mongooses, and smuggled them out to sell to other planters. In this way they quickly spread over the island.

Two mongooses—they killed the rats but didn't stop there.

The mongoose smuggling did not cut into Mr. Espeut's supply very much. For his mongooses did not spend all their time killing rats. They were also busy doing something mongooses do quite well: making more mongooses. A mother mongoose usually has two babies at a time, and she can have two litters in a year.

For a time it seemed that the mongoose was exactly what the Jamaicans had hoped for. Enthusiastic plantation owners shipped mongooses to Cuba, Puerto Rico, Barbados, and other rat-troubled islands, including some of the islands of Hawaii. Soon the furry ratcatchers were well established in those places, too.

But as the rat population decreased, the mongooses turned to other foods. They ate lizards, frogs, crabs, and snakes. They preyed on quail and doves that nested on the ground. They nearly wiped out a little native rodent, the capromys, and greedily devoured the eggs that sea turtles laid on the Jamaican beaches. Mongooses stole chickens and eggs from poultry yards and henhouses. Kittens and puppies, piglets, lambs, and kids were not safe from them. They even ate fruit and vegetables in the farms and gardens. The mongoose had become a pest!

In 1883, the Jamaican government passed laws forbidding any new mongooses to be brought into the island. Bounties were offered for killing these animals that everyone had tried so recently to encourage. But it was too late. The mongoose was firmly established. The same story was repeated on the other islands. In Puerto Rico it was even discovered that the mongoose was spreading rabies, a disease that had never been seen on that island before.

In 1892, there was talk of bringing mongooses into the western United States to get rid of the gophers whose burrows were a nuisance on cattle ranges. Worried scientists protested, and fortunately these plans never came to anything. Today, laws forbid the importation of mongooses into the United States.

The Rabbit Plague

The animals of Australia are unlike those of any other place in the world. There are great leaping kangaroos bounding over the plains. Furry koalas look like living teddy bears and never eat anything but leaves of the eucalyptus tree. There are wallabies, wombats, and creatures that look like cats or mice or moles. But all of them share an unusual trait: they raise their young in a pouch in the mother's belly. They belong to a group called marsupials, from a word meaning pouch. Newborn marsupial babies are very tiny and not well developed. They could not survive out of their mother's pouch.

Two other animals of Australia are even stranger. The duckbill platypus and an anteater called the echidna lay eggs. Yet they are furry and feed their young with milk, just as the other mammals do. These egg-laying mammals are called monotremes.

Scientists believe that once, long before there were humans in the world, the continent of Australia was connected to Asia and Africa, in one big supercontinent. But then this great land mass split apart, and the parts slowly drifted away from each other. Before the continents split apart, all of the mammals were either marsupials or monotremes. Cats and dogs, horses, elephants, mice, and all the other placental mammals—mammals whose young develop longer inside their mother's body before being born—had not appeared yet.

Time went by, long ages of time. On the continents of Asia and Africa, placental mammals appeared. Probably the first ones were small, ratlike creatures. But as the generations went by, every now and then one of their descendants was just a bit different from its parents. And if, by chance, the change made it a little better able to live and thrive, it passed on its new characteristics to its children, and to their children in turn. Gradually all the different kinds of placental mammals developed and spread. Often they were better adapted for survival than the marsupials and monotremes. Gradually, nearly all of these ancient animals disappeared. Only the opossum survived.

But in Australia, somehow the changes that produced the first placental mammal never happened. And while the new mammals spread over the other continents of the world, the vast stretches of ocean that separated the animals from Australia prevented them from reaching its shores. Only a few bats were able to fly from island to island, eventually crossing the Pacific and settling in Australia. Except for the bats, the mammals of Australia remained much the same as they had been long ages before.

The first humans who settled in Australia began to change all that. Brave men in little boats, they reached the great island continent from the smaller islands of the Pacific thousands of years ago. Some settled there and became the aborigines, the first humans in Australia. They took up a life of wandering and food gathering and learned to know and love their land.

The aborigines brought several kinds of mammals with them. They brought dogs to keep them company. Later some of the dogs went wild and became the ancestors of the dingoes, the native Australian dogs. The early settlers did not realize that they also brought some stowaways on their voyages. Hidden in their boats and in their bundles of food and supplies were rats and mice, who eagerly left the boats and settled down in the new land.

Rats and mice, bats and dingoes multiplied and became a part of the Australian wildlife. But for thousands of years, they were the only placental mammals on the island continent.

When British settlers came to Australia at the end of the eighteenth century and later, they brought a number of domestic animals with them. They began raising cattle, pigs, and especially sheep. Many parts of Australia were good grazing lands for sheep, and soon the land "down under" was shipping fine wool all over the world. Even today nearly a third of the world's wool is produced in Australia.

Some of the early settlers brought rabbits with them, and some of these pet rabbits got loose in Sydney and other cities. But apparently these domestic rabbits never

Australia's "native" dog, the dingo, was really an early immigrant.

became pests. There was no rabbit problem in Australia until 1859, when a wealthy landowner named Thomas Austin became homesick for the animals of his native England and ordered a shipment of wild rabbits for his estate.

The European rabbit (*Oryctolagus cuniculus*) belongs to the same general group as the hares and the cottontail rabbits of America. It is about 15 to 18 inches long, with a soft grayish-brown fur coat that helps to camouflage it among the grass and leaves. Wild rabbits live in grasslands and open parts of woodlands. There they dig a maze of underground burrows, which crisscross and connect into a complicated community dwelling place, or warren.

In the center of the warren, in the largest, driest chamber, live the strongest buck and his mate and children. This king buck must fight to win and keep his position. He may permit other males to live in the warren if they acknowledge his leadership. Otherwise they must leave and find a new place of their own. Each dominant buck stakes out a territory, marking the boundaries by "chinning": with special scent glands under his chin he leaves his mark on the ground, plant stems, and other objects along the frontier.

The does (females) do the main work of digging the warren. Each doe also digs a special nest burrow shortly before she gives birth to a litter. The newborn rabbits are naked and helpless, with their eyes and ears tightly shut. Their mother visits them only once each night, to feed them, but they grow quickly. Three weeks after they are born, they are venturing out of the nest burrow to nibble on the grass, and in another week or so they are on their own.

When Thomas Austin thought of bringing rabbits to Australia, he really should have done some checking before he acted. This was not the first of the rabbits' travels, and where they went, they often brought trouble.

Paintings made in Spanish caves by Stone Age men show that rabbits were living there before the time of written history. Phoenician traders, who sailed to Spain around 1000 B.C., picked up some rabbits and helped to spread them to other countries around the Mediterranean. Rabbits were so small and easily cared for that they were a convenient source of fresh meat to carry on long ship voyages. The ancient Romans were fond of rabbit hunting and also raised rabbits for food inside walled enclosures. Conquering Roman armies took rabbits along with them to France and other countries of Europe.

Although Thomas Austin thought of rabbits as part of the natural wildlife of the English countryside, rabbits were not introduced into England until after the Norman conquest in 1066. Wherever they were taken—Italy, France, England, and other countries of Europe—rabbits were prized by many as good animals for hunting. Some domesticated varieties were raised as food animals and pets. (All the rabbits sold today as pets and laboratory animals are descendants of the European rabbit.) But sometimes they multiplied so rapidly that they became serious pests, who raided farmers' crops and ate up the food of grazing animals such as sheep and cattle. Rabbit burrows undermined the ground and made holes for horses and cattle to step into. However, in most places, predators such as weasels and foxes, kept the rabbits in check.

The effects of rabbit invaders were far different in areas where there were no effective predators to keep the rabbit population down. Portuguese sailors, for example, turned some of their ship rabbits loose on the island of Porto Santo in 1418. Perhaps they thought the rabbits would multiply on the island and provide them with a ready meat supply whenever they stopped there. If that was the sailors' plan, it succeeded at first beyond their wildest dreams. There were no natural predators on Porto Santo, and it seemed a rabbit paradise. A wild rabbit can mate when she is only six months old. Within a month she can give birth to a litter of half a dozen or more, and then she can mate again immediately. Before long, the island of Porto Santo was covered with rabbits. The rabbits ate and mated and made more rabbits. There was nothing to stop them until they ran out of food. They ate everything green that grew on the island, and turned Porto Santo into a wasteland. Finally the humans who lived on the island gave up and abandoned it to the rabbits.

The rabbit invasion of Porto Santo happened long before the British immigrants settled in Australia. Yet surely there was no danger of the same thing happening there. Australia is an island, to be sure, but it is so much larger —a whole continent!

In December of 1859, the ship *Lightning* docked in Australia with a shipment for Thomas Austin: two dozen wild rabbits, straight from England. As soon as they

The rabbits in Australia multiplied and multiplied.

reached Mr. Austin's estate in Victoria province, he turned them loose, and the rabbits promptly proceeded to do what rabbits know how to do best. Mr. Austin had hoped his new rabbits would be good hunting some day, but he never expected them to multiply so quickly. Six years later he estimated that he had killed 20,000 rabbits —and probably had about 10,000 left!

At first, Mr. Austin's neighbors were jealous of his rabbit hunting. But they did not have long to wait. In a few years, some of the rabbits had spread out beyond the boundaries of the Austin estate. They found new homes and multiplied, and their children and their children's children moved onward. Across the continent they spread. Rabbit hunting soon became big business, and rabbit fur and meat became major items of export for Australia. For a while nearly everyone was delighted with the new addition to the Australian wildlife.

But the rabbits were doing too well in their new home. There were few natural predators on the island continent, and sheep raisers ruthlessly killed the few there were—the Tasmanian wolf and the dingo—to keep their stock safe. Yet the innocent-seeming rabbits were a far greater danger to the sheep raising industry. Rabbits and sheep eat the same things: grass and other plant life. Both, if they are hungry enough, will eat grass right down to its roots, so that it cannot grow back and dies. A wise sheep raiser can protect his pasture lands by moving his herds before they can cause irreparable damage to the grass. But what can he do about multiplying wild rabbits?

What to do about the rabbits quickly became a burning question in Australia. They were stripping the grasses and turning large areas into a wasteland. Sheep raisers had to reduce their herds because the pastures could not support both sheep and rabbits. Ten little rabbits can eat as much as one sheep!

An enormous campaign was mounted to exterminate the rabbits. But such a campaign could be successful only if *all* the rabbits were killed. (Only twenty-four rabbits began the whole rabbit plague in the first place.) This might have been accomplished by killing the rabbits when they gathered around waterholes during the long droughts. Yet few Australians were entirely sure they wanted *all* the rabbits gone from the land. The average man (if he was not a sheep raiser) thought of these long-eared animals as a handy source of food and extra pocket money.

The government tried. Bounties were offered for rabbit tails, and millions were collected. But still the rabbits kept multiplying. Soon it was noticed that tailless rabbits were hopping about the countryside. Were they a new variety of *Oryctolagus cuniculus,* like the Manx cat? Hardly. They were merely the result of the greed of the trappers, who cut off the tails of the rabbits they caught to turn in for the bounty—then let the rabbits go to breed new bounties for the next year.

In 1901, a desperate effort was begun. If the Australians could not kill all the rabbits, perhaps they could at least limit them to the lands they had already conquered. So they began to build a rabbit fence across the country. The bottom of the fence was buried under the ground so the rabbits could not burrow under it, and the top was strung with barbed wire. It took years to build, and cost more than a million dollars. Eventually it stretched for more than 2,000 miles. But it didn't work. One hole in the fence, just a few inches wide, is enough to let a group of rabbits through to new lands. The famous rabbit fence slowed their advance a bit, but it did not stop the rabbit invaders. What was needed was a foolproof solution, which would work whether all the people really wanted it to or not.

The beginning of the answer was discovered four years before the rabbit fence was begun, but it took half a century to put it into practice. Back in 1897, scientists in the hospital in Montevideo, Uruguay, had noticed that all their laboratory rabbits were dying mysteriously. The disease that killed them was named myxomatosis. The disease does not affect humans, but it is very common among the cottontail rabbits of Brazil and other parts of South America. These wild rabbits have natural defenses against myxomatosis, and the disease is only a mild illness for them. But for European rabbits, who belong to an entirely different species, myxomatosis brings death. Many years of study finally established that myxomatosis is a virus disease that was transferred from the cottontail rabbits to the domestic rabbits in the Montevideo hospital on the mouthparts of mosquitoes who bit the rabbits.

Now scientists had a means of killing rabbits without killing other animals, and a suggestion of a way to spread the disease. After a series of experiments sponsored by Australian government agencies, the virus was introduced into Australia in 1950—and it spread like wildfire. Rabbits died by the millions, and the land began to turn green again.

A French scientist, Dr. Armand Delille, read about the success of the rabbit extermination program in Australia and decided to try the virus on the rabbits that were overrunning his estate at Dreux, near Paris. By that time rabbits had become serious pests in various countries of Europe, as a result of intensive programs for exterminating predators. Dr. Delille obtained some of the virus from a bacteriologist friend, caught two of the rabbits running loose on his estate, and injected them with the virus. Within six weeks, nearly all the wild rabbits on the

How to get rid of the rabbits? (Above) workers test a carbon-monoxide impregnated foam that is pumped into the rabbit burrows. (Below) a highly magnified picture of the myxomatosis virus.

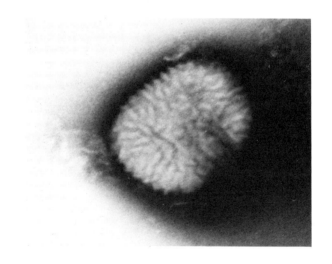

Delille estate were dead.

Dr. Delille had tried to make certain that the results of his experiment would not spread beyond his own estate. His lands were surrounded by a high stone wall, and before he introduced the virus, he made all the gates in the wall rabbit proof. But soon his neighbors heard about his success and begged for supplies of the virus to get rid of their own rabbit pests. When Dr. Delille refused, the neighbors broke into the estate one night and carried off some sick rabbits.

That was in 1952. Within months myxomatosis had spread through France and into Germany, carried by mosquitoes and rabbit fleas. In a year it had crossed the Channel into England. Before long the European rabbit was nearly wiped out in those countries—to the sorrow of rabbit hunters and the delight of farmers.

Meanwhile, in Australia the battle is not yet over. In recent years there have been signs that the myxoma virus may be changing to less potent forms. And rabbits with a natural resistance to myxomatosis are beginning to multiply. Scientists are working on new approaches, such as breeding stronger viruses and developing means of spreading them through fleas. (Mosquitoes do not thrive in some regions of Australia, where the climate is very dry.) One of the newest lines of study is an investigation into the possibility of using artificial chemicals resembling the rabbits' chin scents to ring farms and grazing lands with chemical "no trespassing signs."

New Homes on the Range

Mustangs have a large and important place in United States history. These sturdy wild horses, which roamed the western plains in huge herds, can live on extremely limited supplies of food and water. The plains Indians caught and tamed mustangs and used them for buffalo hunting and raids on settlers. The settlers in turn found the mustang herds a ready supply of transportation in their westward journey.

Yet the mustangs were not originally natives of the United States. Although scientists believe the horse (*Equus caballus*) evolved to its present form from a little, cat-sized ancestor in North America, horses became extinct on this continent more than 8,000 years ago. Only the horses, which had migrated to Asia and Europe survived, and were eventually domesticated by man. The ancestors of the American mustangs were tame horses, brought to this country from Europe about 400 years ago by various Spanish conquistadores. At the end of their travels on the continent, these explorers turned their horses loose to live and multiply on the local fodder. They hoped that when they returned on later voyages, they would find a supply of horses waiting for them.

The mustangs were far more successful than the conquistadores. The western prairies and plains provided plenty of food and living space. The domesticated horses quickly went back to the ways of their wild ancestors. They lived in little bands, each ruled by a stallion who fought to win and keep his leadership and his harem of mares. The mustangs multiplied and spread through the West. It is estimated that by 1870 there were 3.5 million of them roaming the western grasslands.

The mustang—a legacy of the conquistadores.

But as the West was settled, people began to use the grasslands for grazing cattle and sheep. Domesticated horses became plentiful and it was easier to buy a horse than to catch and tame members of the wary mustang herds. The mustangs also competed with deer and antelopes that the new settlers enjoyed hunting. So men began slaughtering the mustang herds, leaving the bodies to rot or using them for dogmeat. As cars and trucks, and later airplanes, became common, it grew easier and easier to track down and kill the wild horses. Now it is believed that there are only about 16,000 left, scattered over 11 western states. There are a few preserves where mustangs roam under the protection of the United States government. But elsewhere the slaughter continues. This animal invader has had its time of glory and soon may vanish forever.

Meanwhile the American West has become the scene of a series of animal invasions unparalleled by anything since Noah's ark. Barbary sheep, originally natives of North Africa, now roam free in Texas and New Mexico. They have found the canyons of these western states a welcome home and are thriving. But wildlife experts are worried about what effect they may have on our native bighorn sheep.

Wildlife officials in New Mexico, searching for new game animals to add to their state's resources, have also brought over the Siberian ibex, a relative of the domestic goat; the greater kudu, a type of antelope from Africa, the males of which bear a pair of enormous twisted horns;

Exotics on the range—a Siberian ibex.

An eland.

and the oryx, an antelope with a pair of long, pointed horns.

In Texas, ranchers have imported a fantastic variety of exotic animals from Asia and Africa. Zebras and elands, black bucks and mouflon sheep, axis deer and nilgai mingle with champion cattle. In a survey in 1964, wildlife biologists counted thirteen different kinds of imported ungulates (hoofed animals) in Texas alone.

The importers of these animals point out, quite rightly, that some of them are in real danger of extinction in their native homes. In Africa, for example, kudu are being slaughtered so rapidly that there may soon be none left. In a way, then, the growing herds of foreign wildlife in the American West may really serve as a sort of Noah's ark, saving animals whose descendants may one day be returned to their native homes. But what will happen in the meantime to the native deer, antelopes, and bighorn sheep who must share their habitat with the newcomers? What other effects may these imported ungulates have on the wildlife communities of the American West? Some wildlife biologists, thinking of the lessons of the past, are worried.

In Alaska, for example, settlers found reindeer moss growing thickly on the tundra. But there were no reindeer. So in 1891 the United States government began importing reindeer from Siberia. It was thought that the reindeer would thrive on the Alaskan tundra and provide a new source of meat for the Eskimo who lived there.

At first the experiment seemed a success. By 1940, there were more than a quarter of a million reindeer living in herds in Alaska. But then the numbers of the reindeer began to shrink. In 1950, only 25,000 of them remained.

What had happened? It took some time to sort out all the causes, and even now the picture is somewhat confused. Part of the problem lay in the fact that the Eskimos were not used to being herders, and they found it hard to change their ways. Some reindeer were killed by packs of wolves, which attacked the roaming herds. And furthermore, the reindeer moss, which had seemed so perfect for the reindeer, grows so slowly that it may take more than a quarter of a century for it to be replaced once it is eaten. When there were too many reindeer, they ate this natural fodder too quickly, and then there was not enough food to support the large herds.

Two reindeer from the Kotzebue herd in Alaska with their Eskimo herder.

An imported ungulate brought a different kind of problem to New Zealand. During the second half of the nineteenth century, homesick English settlers sent for red deer from their old home. In New Zealand the transplanted deer did too well. They multiplied and began to raid farmers' crops and damage forests with their browsing. They ate the plant cover that helps to keep the soil from washing away in the rains, and serious erosion resulted. The deer became so crowded, that even they suffered. Many of them were puny and sickly, and hunters missed the magnificent antlers of the past. Finally New Zealand declared an open season on the red deer and further encouraged hunters by offering them free ammunition. Even with these measures, the government must still employ more than a hundred hunters, who work full time to keep the deer in check.

In spite of these discouraging examples, ungulates continue to travel from country to country. Deer and antelopes are imported from Asia and Africa to the United States and to Britain and other European countries. Some of them do not take well to their new homes and die out. Some prosper and become valuable additions to the native wildlife. And some do so well that people wish they had stayed at home.

The Case of the Walking Catfish and Other Fish Stories

Long, long ago, when the world was younger, scientists believe, all of the animals and plants lived in the sea. The lands were rocky and bare. But as the long ages of time went by, the wind and weather began the process of turning the rocks to soil. First a few, then many plants, blown by the winds or splashed up by the waves, took root on the dry lands and flourished and spread. Where there were plants, there was food. After a few million years or so, the first animals ventured onto the lands. Insects came, and then some fish found that they, too, could live part of their lives on the land.

Perhaps the first fish invaders lived in shallow pools that dried up in times of drought. Perhaps a few fish, which were born just a bit different from the other fish in the sea, were able to gasp and sputter enough in the air to keep them alive while they dragged themselves from their drying pool to another, deeper one. Perhaps in time other fish were born, with stronger fins that were better for getting around on land. And some of them had lungs, so that they could take oxygen from the air just as their ancestors had gathered it in from the water.

In time, the scientists believe, the descendants of these fish became true amphibians, able to live both in water and on the land. In time, true land animals developed: reptiles, and then birds and mammals.

If all these theories about the evolution of life on earth are correct, we should be thankful that some of these early fish ancestors made the change to life on land—otherwise we humans would never have existed. But people in Florida and a growing number of other parts of the United States are rapidly coming to wish that one kind of fish had never thought of leaving its watery home. This animal invader is the walking catfish (*Clarias batrachus*).

As with so many animal invaders, a little foresight might have avoided the whole problem. But the fish dealer who had the bright idea of breeding his own supplies of these tropical fish was not thinking ahead—or perhaps he did not realize just what the walking catfish can do.

Clarias batrachus looks pretty much like other catfish. It has a large, broad head with "whiskers" and a long, eellike body. It grows to be about 16 inches long, and weighs about a pound when full grown.

Walking catfish have three unusual features to recommend them to people who keep tropical fish. First, they are one of the few fish that are ever found in nature in albino forms. The usual color for *Clarias batrachus* is a grayish or dirty brown black, with a somewhat lighter belly. But the albinos have a creamy white skin and pink

The walking catfish—the "fish that got away."

eyes. Their second unusual feature is a pair of large air chambers behind their gills—somewhat like a simple pair of lungs. In ponds, walking catfish can often be seen coming up to the surface to gulp in some air. Indeed, fish raisers have found that these fish cannot breathe in the water as well as other fish can. In developing a kind of lungs, they have lost part of the use of their gills. If they are placed in a fish tank with a floating glass cover, so that they cannot get oxygen from the air above the water, they die.

The third unusual thing about the walking catfish is the one that gave the fish its name: it can walk on dry land. Actually, the fish do not walk very well. What they do resembles a man crawling along on his elbows. The fish have two pectoral fins, each with a strong, tough spine on the front. In "walking," the fish balances on one of its spines, arches its back, drags its tail forward, and then flops out full length. It gains only a few inches by this maneuver, but if the ground is wet it can cover 4 or 5 feet in a minute. And it can stay out of the water for as much as 24 hours, as long as the ground is damp enough to keep its skin from drying out.

It is not hard to understand why the walking catfish was a favorite of tropical fish fanciers who enjoyed having an "oddity" in their collection. For some time, the demand was supplied by imports from Bangkok, Thailand, and other parts of Southeast Asia. The fish could be bought for only thirty-nine cents each. But then walking catfish appeared on television, on the Johnny Carson Show and various others. People all over the country suddenly decided they must have some of these unusual fish. And *Clarias batrachus* began to sell for nine or ten dollars each.

A tropical fish importer in Boca Raton, Florida, decided that it would be much simpler and more profitable to raise his own walking catfish. So he placed some in a holding pond, where he kept and bred some varieties of fish. That was an expensive mistake for the fish dealer. Perhaps he did not realize that walking catfish find other fish good eating. They promptly ate up all the other fish in the pond. Then they got hungry. Before the fish dealer realized what had happened, the walking catfish had leaped out of his pond (they can jump up to 4 feet) and walked off in search of a better home.

Florida was a paradise for the walking catfish. It is rather warm all year-round (walking catfish cannot live in water below 50 degrees), and it has many swamps and bodies of water, linked together by a network of canals. There are plenty of fish and shellfish for the catfish to eat, and if it gets hungry on its overland travels, it can eat frogs, snails, insects, or even weeds and roots. In time of drought, the fish can either jump out of its pond and go looking for another one, or it can burrow down into the mud and wait for rain. (It can live that way for weeks.)

No one realized at first that the walking catfish were loose, or that they were doing so well. The original fish from the breeder's pond spawned in the warm Florida waters, and soon one generation followed another. Probably the catfish population was also increased by fish owners who got tired of their pets and dumped them into the nearest pond or canal. In 1968, the first wild walking catfish was noticed, flopping along the road near Boca Raton. In the next year, more than 3,000 of them were caught. Fishermen found the fish could be hooked on worms, cheese, bread, and insects. They are good eating, too—just as tasty as the native American catfish, although harder to skin.

At first all the walking catfish that were caught were albinos, like the ones that had escaped from the fish importer's pond. But soon some fish with the natural gray color were spotted, and their numbers grew as time went on. This finding, and the fact that some of the walking catfish were young ones, called attention to the fact that *Clarias batrachus* was spawning successfully in the Florida waters.

Why is everyone so worried about the walking catfish? What difference does it make if one more fish is added to the Florida wildlife? The problem is that the catfish is such a greedy fish. It gobbles up so many minnows and other small fish that there is not enough food left for other larger fish. When walking catfish move into a pond or canal, they are soon the only kind of fish there. And when there is no food left, the walking catfish simply jump out and move on.

When Florida officials realized that *Clarias batrachus* had established itself in the wilds, they quickly tried to catch all the catfish that were loose. But it was too late. There were already too many of them. State fishery researchers tried to think of ways to kill the catfish. They found that the insecticide rotenone kills the fish. But attempts to use the poison in practice were a dismal failure. Perhaps rotenone would have worked if the walking catfish had cooperated. But as soon as the poison began to bother them, they jumped out of the water and walked away, leaving the other fish in the pond to die. Now researchers are trying to find some parasite or disease or natural enemy of the walking catfish that might be used to control them without killing off other fish.

It is now against the law to buy, sell, or import *Clarias batrachus* or its eggs anywhere in the United States. But the walking catfish that are already here have spread all over Florida and to southern Georgia. Experts fear that it is only a matter of time before they are established in Texas and other states with a warm, hospitable climate.

The walking catfish is not the first "fish that got away" —nor is it likely to be the last. Tropical fish are big business in the United States, and raising them is a hobby that has brought many hours of pleasure to millions of people. But some people find that raising them is too much trouble, or grow tired of their pets. Others find that their fish give birth to more young fish than they have room for. They cannot bear the thought of killing the fish. Wouldn't it be much kinder to give them a chance for life in a nearby pond or stream?

Dumping pet tropical fish into handy ponds and streams does not do much harm in most parts of the country. The fish are used to warm water, and as soon as the weather turns cold, they die. But in the warm southern states they have a chance to survive. And Florida has had more than its share of problems.

Fish biologists at the University of Miami have estimated that at least thirty different kinds of foreign fish have already established themselves in Florida waters. At least eight species of the cichlid family are now living wild. These brightly colored fish from Latin America and Africa are favorites with aquarium owners. But in natural waters they compete for food and space with the young of valuable food and game fish, such as tarpon, bass, and sunfish. Tourists are an important source of income for the state of Florida, and one thing tourists come to Florida to do is fish. If the walking catfish, cichlids, and other imported fish reduce the numbers of the good sport fish, the Florida tourist industry will suffer a serious loss.

Another imported fish in Florida is causing a different kind of trouble. The pike killifish comes from Yucatán in Mexico, where it lives in its own, nicely adjusted water community. Killifishes are a favorite with tropical fish fans because their eggs take a long time (up to two weeks) to hatch. This means that fish raisers can trade eggs by air mail with pen pals all over the world. But in Florida waters, pike killifish feed on mosquitofish, and those useful little fish eat insects. Thus pike killifish may be helping to spread mosquitoes in Florida.

Worrisome as these problems are, there is one other imported fish whose name alone is enough to make Florida officials turn pale. That is the piranha.

The piranha does not look like a very dangerous fish. One of the most common species (*Serrasalmus nattereri*) rarely grows to be as much as a foot long, and the piranhas kept by tropical fish fanciers are usually much smaller.

But the piranha has a mouth full of razor-sharp teeth and a jaw so strong that it can easily bite off a person's finger, bones and all! This little fish has a disposition to match his weapons. Fish raisers must keep piranhas separate, one to a tank. They will fiercely attack not only other kinds of fish, both large and small, but even other piranhas. In the Amazon and Orinoco Rivers of South America, their natural home, piranhas live in schools of a hundred or more. They normally feed on smaller fish, but if a large animal happens to fall into the water—particularly if it is bleeding—they will not hesitate to attack it. Tearing out chunks of flesh, a school of piranhas can strip an animal to a skeleton in less than a minute.

The piranha—small but deadly.

In an aquarium by itself, a piranha is less bold, but it can still give its owner a nasty bite if it is handled. Understandably, there are not many tropical fish raisers who care to have such a dangerous pet. But piranhas look very much like other members of their family, such as the silver dollar fish. They are often brought into the country accidentally with these and other more popular fish. Florida officials live with the constant nightmare that piranhas may at some time become established in the state. And there is already evidence that they could survive and thrive in the Florida climate. In 1970, agents of the Florida Game and Fresh Water Fish Commission captured some piranhas in the swimming pool of a home in West Miami. The owner had placed them there the year before. (Obviously he did not care very much for swimming!) They had survived one of the coldest winters in recent Miami history.

Early the following year, a fisherman pulled a piranha out of a canal near Boca Raton. (Piranhas are good eating, but they usually bite right through a fisherman's line and swim away before he can bring them in.) The fisherman called the local game officials, and they immediately sped to the scene and poisoned a half-mile stretch of the canal.

Most of the imported fish that are now troubling Florida waters were introduced accidentally. But some were put there on purpose. The Florida Game and Fresh Water Fish Commission itself was responsible for introducing *Tilapia*. Members of the cichlid family, most *Tilapia* species belong to a group called mouthbreeders. When a pair are ready to breed, the male digs a hole in the sand or mud at the bottom. He coaxes the female to lay her eggs there. Then, after the male has fertilized the eggs, the female scoops them up in her mouth. She will hold them carefully in her mouth until they hatch—as much as three weeks, depending on the kind of *Tilapia* and the temperature. During this time she will not eat—and she is very careful not to swallow the eggs! Even after the little fish hatch, their mother keeps them in her mouth for a while. And when they venture out into the world of the pond, they quickly dive back into Mama's mouth if there is a threat of danger.

In their African home, *Tilapia* and other cichlids are considered good food fishes. They feed on tiny shellfish and other small water animals, and also nibble on water plants. So Florida game officials thought *Tilapia* would be a good game fish and would help to control the growth of weeds. Unfortunately, it was a while before they discovered that they had brought in the wrong *Tilapia*. The species they had was not a good game fish at all. And by that time the fish were well established and threatening to take over large sections of South and Central Florida completely.

Attempts to improve on nature's fish distribution continue. In 1971, it was discovered that the white amur (*Ctenopharyngodon idella*) was loose in the White River, a tributary of the Mississippi. This fish, a member of the carp family, comes from eastern Asia. There its meat is prized as a delicacy. Three feet long and weighing up to 70 pounds, the white amur swims and jumps so strongly that sportsmen love it. It eats mainly waterweeds, especially the algae that can choke lakes and kill all their animal life when it gets out of hand.

In our modern world, algae growing in lakes creates a real problem. Nitrates and phosphates from fertilizers that farmers use on their fields are carried by rain into streams that feed the lakes. More phosphorus and nitrogen compounds are carried into the natural waters with sewage from homes and industry. (Phosphates are a key ingredient in most modern detergents, and human wastes are rich in both nitrogen and phosphorus.) In a lake, these chemicals act as fertilizers, sparking a rich growth of algae, which may then cover the whole surface of the lake with a coat of green. But the algae cannot go on growing forever. When the small plants die, they sink and decompose, using up the oxygen dissolved in the water. Deprived of the oxygen, the fish and other water animals die too. Eventually the whole lake dies.

White amurs are like living vacuum cleaners, eating up to four times their own weight in algae each day. Enthusiastic scientists in the United States Bureau of Sport Fisheries imported seventy of the fish from Malaysia in 1963 and turned them over to the Arkansas Game and Fish Commission. The test areas were carefully fenced off with wire mesh, but apparently some holes must have developed, since the fish turned up in the White River. Eight years of testing had gone on before the white amurs were discovered in the White River, and in that time the Asian carp had looked very promising. So since the fish were loose anyway, scientists decided in 1972 to stock fifteen Arkansas lakes with thousands of them.

Only time will tell if the white amurs will fulfill their promise as lake cleaners and game fish or if they will turn out to be another animal transplanters' mistake. Scientists are hopeful, but they are still cautious. They remember what happened a century ago, when hopeful scientists brought another member of the same family, the European carp, to America. Enthusiastic fish raisers quickly spread the carp to ponds, lakes, and streams all over the country, and they thrived and multiplied. Too late it was found that they are not very good sport fish and are not as tasty as it had been thought. Even worse, they have a habit of rooting around on the bottom for plant life, which muddies the water and ruins it for plant growth and for other fish.

A century has gone by, and scientists still have not found an answer to the European carp. Unless they can find or make chemicals that will kill only certain kinds of fish and leave all others alone, it seems that the carp and the other imported fish are here to stay.

The Creeping Menace: The Giant African Snail

An eight-year-old boy was responsible for one of the newest threats to United States wildlife and agriculture. In 1966, the boy was taken on a vacation trip to Hawaii. There he found three pretty land snails, with pointed brown-and-white striped shells. They were fun to play with, and just the right size to fit into his pockets. So he took them home with him.

Back home in North Miami, the boy's mother discovered the snails. She did not want slimy animals in the house, even if they did have pretty shells. She told her son to get rid of them, and he let them go in the backyard.

No one realized, at first, that the giant African snail (*Achatina fulica*) had finally slipped through the nation's defenses and established a beachhead on the mainland.

Three snails might seem like a rather small invading party. But three snails can multiply very quickly. Land snails are hermaphrodites: each one has the reproductive organs of both a male and a female. A snail cannot have babies by itself, but when two snails mate, each one can shortly become a mother. And a single mating may be enough for a lifetime. A snail can store the sperms that it receives from its mate inside its body and use them to fertilize the eggs of its next clutch, too, months later.

The giant African snail lays eggs—up to five hundred of them at a time—in damp soil every two or three months. Inside each pearly egg, about the size of a BB shot, the new life grows quickly. The baby snails, miniature copies of their parents, hatch in ten days or less.

Each snail has its body coiled inside a long, pointed shell. If it lives to the ripe old age of five years or more, it may be fully 8 inches long and weigh a pound.

When danger threatens, the snail can pull its whole body into the safety of its shell. But when it is active and undisturbed, it puts out a head and a large, muscular foot. Mounted on top of the snail's head, like TV antennae, are two pairs of pointed "horns" or tentacles, two large ones and two small ones. At the tip of each of the large tentacles is a round eye. The small tentacles hold other sense organs. The snail waves them about, testing and probing its environment for signs of food or danger. The ends of two long tentacles may seem like a rather vulnerable place to keep a pair of eyes. But the snail can protect its organs of sight by pulling them in, turning its tentacles inside out like the fingers of a glove.

Rippling the strong muscles of its foot, the snail glides slowly along in a trail of slime that is made inside its body. The giant African snail does not have gills, as sea snails do. Instead, it breathes with a "lung" cavity inside its body. Water, which it needs, is easily lost through its soft, moist skin, but this does not cause the snail any trouble. If the weather turns dry, and there is not enough water around to replace what is lost, the snail pulls back into its shell and seals off the opening with a thin membrane. It enters a sleeplike state called estivation. It can stay this way, barely breathing and not eating at all, for a whole year. When moisture comes again, it will poke its head and foot out of its shell and take up life again.

The giant African snail is a very efficient "eating machine." It has a long, ribbonlike tongue called a radula. Along the outer surface of the radula are numerous rows of tiny cutting teeth—80,000 of them! The snail uses its radula to rasp off bits of food and slide them, like a conveyor belt, into its mouth.

Achatina fulica is not very particular about its diet. It feeds on rotting plant materials and the bodies of dead animals. It also gorges itself greedily on leaves, fruits, bark, and flowers of living plants. A single snail can run through a whole head of lettuce overnight. Giant African snails can do terrible damage to a field of beans or cabbage, or an orchard of citrus trees. But these foods may not provide the snails with enough calcium to build their limy shells. So they may climb the walls of houses, eating the whitewash and paint.

Usually the giant African snails feed at dusk or at night. But when it is rainy or overcast, they may come out during the daytime as well. They are active only when the temperature is above 75 degrees. When it turns cold, they creep deep into a hollow log or under a stone

The giant African snail traveled a long road to Miami.

and hibernate, remaining still until it is warm again.

With these habits and abilities and few natural enemies, *Achatina fulica* seems like a sure bet to survive in the warm climate and lush vegetation of Florida. And so it is not surprising that within a couple of years, Miami officials were getting complaints of damage from snail pests. Large snails were eating up garden plants and rasping the paint off the fronts of houses. By 1969, it was estimated that there were 20,000 giant African snails in a single thirteen-square-block area!

A massive campaign was launched. Poison baits containing arsenic were spread for the snails. But soon it was discovered that the baits were also killing the giant snails' main natural enemy, the tiny cannibal snail, which attacks and eats the big snails. The efforts of state and federal agriculture workers to find and gather the snails and their eggs by hand met with a number of difficulties. During the day, the snails rest in cool, moist hiding places, such as cracks in the foundations of houses, and even inside air conditioners. Looking for snails at night through the backyards of the neighborhood had its own hazards: barking and biting watchdogs.

In spite of all these difficulties, by the summer of 1971 Florida officials believed they had the giant snail problem licked. But then, after a long drought, followed by flooding rains, the snails reappeared in a different Miami neighborhood. Agriculture department workers believe that the spread of the pest is being helped by school busing. Children love to play with the snails and carry pet snails in their pockets. When they attend schools in other neighborhoods, they carry *Achatina fulica* with them.

If the giant African snail has indeed successfully established itself in Miami, snail experts fear that it will spread throughout the southern states, from the Carolinas to Southern California. Officials believe that it could cause $11 million a year in damage to crops in Florida alone.

The story of the giant African snail's successful invasion of the United States mainland is only the latest chapter in a long history of continent-hopping. The snail is a native of East Africa. In its original home, it is not a serious pest. In fact, it is an important food animal. Its numbers are held in check by a number of predators—insects, other snail species, crabs, and civet cats. But these predators have not followed *Achatina fulica* in its travels around the world, and in many new homes it found few natural enemies.

The travels of the giant African snail began around 1800. The wife of the governor of Mauritius was ill, and her doctor believed a substance found in the snails might help her. Snails were brought over from Africa and multiplied quickly. Soon they were busily rasping away at the Mauritius cotton crop. Some of the snails were carried to nearby islands, but the next big jump did not come until 1847. A traveling Englishman saw the snails on a visit to Mauritius. He collected a few as souvenirs, but at the next stop on his journey decided not to keep them. He deposited the snails in the botanical gardens in Calcutta, India. There they multiplied and prospered.

By the end of the century, the snails had spread from India to Ceylon and were damaging the cacao plants. On, the snails advanced. Sometimes they were spread accidentally, while they were estivating in bananas or in motor vehicles. Sometimes they were introduced into a new area on purpose. In 1928, for example, they were brought to Sarawak to be used as poultry feed. In neighboring Malaya, the giant snails were soon devastating rubber plantations. A few short hops took them to Singapore and Java, and soon to the Far East as well.

In 1936, a young woman from Hawaii picked up two giant African snails on a visit to Formosa. She smuggled them past the port inspectors and placed them in her garden because she thought they were so pretty. In the same year, a man in Maui had some snails mailed to him from Japan. Hawaiian officials did not discover the invasions until two years later—and by then it was too late. *Achatina fulica* was already a thriving resident of Hawaii.

The next big advance came during World War II. The Japanese had become fond of the meat of the big snails, and they brought them to several Pacific Islands as food animals. When American soldiers moved into Saipan, they found snails clinging to the trees and slithering through the grass and across highways. Dead snails and slime trails made the roads slippery and dangerous. Live snails, attracted to the bodies of the dead ones, were squashed by the highway traffic and added to the stinking mess. Flies bred in the slime and spread disease. The rat poison warfarin was used to try to get rid of the pests, but the snails thrived on it instead. They were so eager to get more of the poison that they kept springing traps that were meant to catch rats.

On the Micronesian Islands, east of the Philippines, the giant African snail played a role in an amazing series of events that clearly illustrate how unexpected results may follow man's attempts to tamper with nature's balances. Rats were a problem on the islands. Someone remembered that in Japan the giant monitor lizard eats rats. Giant monitor lizards were brought in and released before it was realized that rats are usually active at night, while the lizards are daytime animals. Soon the lizards were slipping into henhouses and eating chickens and eggs.

Now it occurred to someone that the lizards also feed on the giant toad (*Bufo marinus*), the same creature that was introduced into Jamaica to eat red ants. These toads were brought in, and soon the lizards were feeding on them instead of the chickens. But the toads have poison glands, and soon the lizards began to die off. This seemed like a fine result until it was discovered that the lizards had been eating the grubs of the rhinoceros beetle, which damages coconut palms. They had also been eating the coconut crab, which had been feeding on giant African snails.

As the lizards died off, the toads multiplied. Pigs ate them and died. Dogs and cats were poisoned by the toads, too. And then the rats, which the dogs and cats had been eating, multiplied more than before. Meanwhile, the giant snails, which were also multiplying, fed on the dead bodies of the dogs and cats, and the natives blamed them for the death of their pets.

When World War II was over, jeeps, tanks, and other military vehicles were shipped back from the Pacific Islands. They all had to be scalded with live steam to kill the snails and other pests hidden in nooks and crannies inside. A few giant African snails reached California alive, but they were caught and killed. For a while the mainland was safe.

The next challenge came in 1948, when a man in Baltimore bought a giant African snail and kept it as a pet. It escaped but was recaptured. Soon after that it laid a mass of eggs, but they did not hatch. Nearly twenty years later, successful invaders slipped into Miami in the pocket of an eight-year-old boy.

Insect Friends and Foes

The authors were once working on a project that involved raising cotton aphids. We received a shipment of these tiny insects from an agricultural research station in Texas, together with ten pounds of cottonseeds to use for growing food for the aphids. When we opened the box of seeds, three brown insects, each about half-an-inch long, suddenly popped out of the box and scampered rapidly away. Fortunately they were quickly recaptured, placed in a jar, and examined to see what manner of exotic stowaway had hitched a ride from the research station. They were German cockroaches.

We were lucky. These insect stowaways were caught and disposed of before they could infest the house. Countless other people have not been so fortunate. Insects are the commonest animal invaders. They travel throughout the world, establishing new homes. Insects hide in clothing, in wood, and in fruit and vegetables. They hitch rides on animal travelers. They skulk in the crevices of cartons and packing materials. Many insects can withstand extremely high or low temperatures, temperatures that would kill human beings and most other animals. Insect eggs may be even hardier.

The United States Department of Agriculture and similar agencies in other countries maintain a constant vigil against insects. They carefully check travelers' baggage and incoming shipments of all kinds of goods for signs of insect stowaways—indications often so small that only an expert could spot them. If items are found to be contaminated, they are either treated to kill the insects or completely destroyed.

An inspection program like this means an enormous cost in time, money, and effort. But it is well worth it. Some insects are extremely specialized. If their own particular food—perhaps a particular kind of tree or animal that is found only in a certain part of the world—is not available, they will quickly die. But many other insects are quite adaptable, able to change their habits to suit changing conditions. If such adaptable insects are transported to a new home, they can become a major pest.

Humans have helped to spread insects around the world since they first began to travel. Descendants of hitchhiking cockroaches can now be found in every country. Puritan settlers brought clothes moths to the New World in their woolen clothes, and these insects have been eating holes in American clothing and housefurnishings ever since. Hessian soldiers returned to Europe after the Revolutionary War, but small gnats that they carried with them in their straw mattresses still plague American wheat

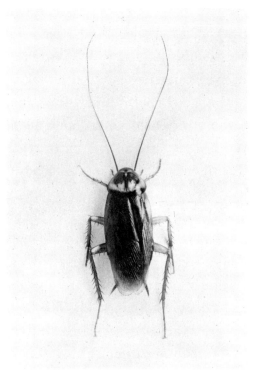

Periplaneta americana, *one of the world-traveling cockroaches.*

farmers. To this day they are called Hessian flies.

Insect invaders still keep coming. People in southeastern United States are now complaining bitterly about fire ants, whose stings are so painful that they sometimes must be treated by a doctor. The red fire ant (*Solenopsis saevissima richteri*) is a relative newcomer to the northern hemisphere. It came to the United States from South America in the early 1900s. At first it spread slowly, but now it threatens most of the southern states.

Like other ants, fire ants live in communities, with a queen ant and a large number of workers. The queen has just one job: to lay eggs that will hatch into new members of the colony. The workers build the colony's home, a large mound of soil and bits of dead plant matter, loosely fastened together. They gather food, tend the eggs and larvae in the nursery, and care for the queen. All the worker ants are females, but they cannot lay eggs of their own.

Some of the young in each group are fertile males and females. Unlike the worker ants, they have wings. When they are full grown, they leave the colony for a mating flight that may cover a distance of ten miles.

After mating, each queen settles down far from her original home to start a new colony. At first she is all alone. She does not eat, but lives on the food stored in her body. She finds some sheltered spot on the ground and settles down to the work of laying eggs. She feeds and cares for the first eggs herself, cleaning and tending them. In a month or less, her labors are rewarded. The first worker ants are grown and ready to do the work of the colony. The queen will never have to do anything but lay eggs ever again.

Fire ants can be a real nuisance in fields and pastures. They sting farm workers and grazing animals, and their mounds, up to 2 feet high, damage mowing machines and other equipment. In cities, fire ants infest lawns, parks, and playgrounds. Their stings can be particularly dangerous for people who are allergic to the ants' poison. Treatment with insecticides can kill the fire ants, but they

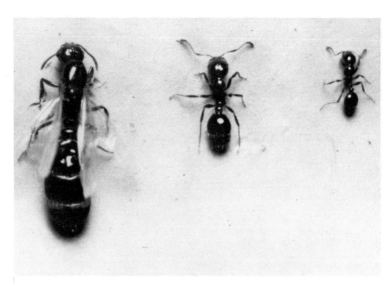

Fire ants. From left to right, a queen, a worker, and a drone.

Fire ants feed on an okra bud.

are already so widespread that a major program will be needed to stop their advance.

Meanwhile, Murray Blum, an insect researcher at the University of Georgia, has been studying the fire ants' poison, which is made in a poison sac in the ant's abdomen. Professor Blum first became interested in fire ants when his young daughter was attacked and stung by several of them. He noticed that the blisters that formed from fire ant stings did not become infected and wondered if the ant poison might have germ-killing properties. Each ant contains such a tiny amount of venom that it took two workers two months to collect enough poison to study. Sure enough, it was found that fire ant venom stops the growth of a number of disease bacteria and molds, and it even kills other insects like houseflies. Perhaps the fire ant story may have a happy ending after all.

Meanwhile, agriculture researchers are still struggling with another foreign insect pest, the elm bark beetle (*Scolytus multistriatus*). This beetle spreads Dutch elm disease, which is killing hundreds of millions of dollars worth of shade trees in thirty eastern and midwestern states. The blight first appeared in the Netherlands in 1921. Efforts were made to try to keep the disease from spreading to other countries, but at first scientists did not know exactly what caused it or how it was spread. In 1930, the disease suddenly appeared in elm trees in Ohio, and it spread quickly to the eastern states. The brown leaves of infected trees mark the advance of the disease.

Years of study revealed the causes of the disease, and now scientists are trying to use their knowledge to fight it. Dutch elm disease is caused by a fungus, which grows inside the tree's water-conducting tubes, choking them and strangling the tree. The fungus is spread from tree to tree by the elm bark beetle, which carries spores of the fungus on its feet. A female beetle lays her eggs in recently cut, broken, or dying elm branches. The grublike larvae that hatch from the eggs tunnel through the wood of the tree, carrying the fungus with them. When they become adults, they emerge from the tree trunks and feed on the bark, often moving to other elm trees that were healthy before they arrived.

One way to control Dutch elm disease is to attack the fungus that causes it. So infected trees are often wrapped with cloth soaked in fungicides, or the chemicals are buried in the ground where the roots of the tree can take them up. Another approach is to kill the beetles that spread the fungus. Chemical insecticides such as DDT have been used with some success. But the DDT used to treat a sick elm tree is taken in by earthworms living in the soil under it. Robins eat the earthworms, and the DDT stays in their bodies. When the birds have taken in enough of the poison, they die.

Scientists realized that one reason Dutch elm disease has spread so quickly is that the elm bark beetle has no natural enemies in the United States. They began a search in Europe for natural enemies of the pest, and came up with a tiny parasitic wasp (*Dendrosoter protuberans*). The larva of this wasp develops on the body of the elm bark beetle larva. It never grows as large as the beetle larva, but like a tiny vampire it sucks the body juices of

Beetles can change a neighborhood. The photo (above) was taken in 1959 in Rumford, Maine. The photo (below) taken in 1966; shows the same street after its shade trees were killed by Dutch elm disease.

the beetle larva and eventually kills it.

Scientists brought some of the wasps to the United States and began to study them. They found that the wasps do not feed on anything but elm-bark beetle larvae. If the wasps succeeded in wiping out the pest, they would die too, and would not become pests themselves.

The parasitic wasps have been released in a number of states whose elms suffer from Dutch elm disease. Meanwhile, Department of Agriculture researchers are working on other approaches, such as efforts to breed new strains of elms, more resistant to the disease.

Like the parasitic wasp that feeds on elm bark beetles, not all the insect invaders that travel from one country to another come uninvited. Sometimes the results have

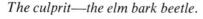

The culprit—the elm bark beetle.

This wasp, Dendrosoter protuberans, *is laying an egg through the bark of an elm tree beside a bark beetle larva hidden under the bark. When the wasp egg hatches, its larva will feed on the beetle larva and kill it.*

been happy ones for everyone. An Australian ladybird beetle, for example, has been transported to California and South Africa to keep the cottony cushion scale from destroying citrus crops. (The insect pest itself was an animal immigrant, which had hitchhiked in from Australia on imported plants.) Meanwhile, when Australians had a problem with the prickly pear cactus, they found the answer in Argentina.

The prickly pear cactus itself was not a native of Australia. It was introduced to that continent from the deserts of the United States during the nineteenth century and quickly took over more than sixty million acres of the best grazing and wheatlands. The prickly spined cacti drove out the native grasses, and people and animals could not even walk through the fields.

At one time, people raised cacti so that they could grow a tiny scale insect that produced a red dye called cochineal. When synthetic dyes were invented, cochineal was no longer very important. But before that happened, all the pests that killed or damaged cacti had been studied very carefully. When the plants were no longer needed, the Australians put their knowledge of pests to use in an effort not to protect their cacti but to get rid of them. They tried more than 150 different insects that feed on cacti, but the prickly pear continued to spread. Finally, in 1925, they tried a little moth from Argentina (*Cactoblastis cactorum*). The larvae of the moth tunnel in the pulpy stems of the cactus. Disease organisms get into the plant through these tunnels, and the cacti die. After the moth was introduced, millions of acres of land were quickly reclaimed and are now producing crops or grasses for grazing sheep. Someone even suggested that the moth should be given a place on the Australian coat of arms.

Like the prickly pear cactus, many other plant invaders have run wild when they have been moved from place to place, leaving their natural enemies behind. And more and more, scientists are turning to natural enemies to control displaced plants. The alligatorweed, for example,

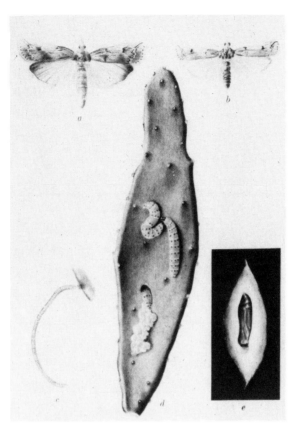

*Imported weapon against the prickly pear cactus—*Cactoblastis cactorum. *Female and male moths are shown in (a) and (b). (c) an eggstick; (d) larvae on a cactus; (e) a cocoon showing a pupa.*

is a water plant from South America, which first appeared in Florida around 1894 and quickly spread to other southern states and California. Few native American water plants can compete successfully with the fast-growing alligatorweed. It crowds out the native plants and chokes the waterways with a green blanket. Drainage canals are blocked, causing flooding. Fish and other wildlife die when the waterweeds crowd out the creatures' normal plant foods and cut down the amount of oxygen in the water. And mosquitoes breed among the spreading weeds.

Cutting or chopping the alligatorweed away just helps to spread it, for every inch or two along the stems there is a node that can develop into a whole new plant. So U.S. Department of Agriculture scientists traveled to South America to search for enemies of the waterweed in Argentina, Brazil, and Paraguay. A number of insects were found on the South American alligatorweeds, and three of the best prospects were brought back for study: the tiny alligatorweed thrips; a moth called the alligatorweed stem borer; and a yellow and black striped beetle called the alligatorweed flea beetle. Careful studies were made to be sure that these insects would feed only on alligatorweeds, and would not become pests by eating something else after they were transplanted. The insects passed their tests and have been let loose in a number of states. The beetle, in particular, is already helping to clear the waterways in many areas. As they eat the alligatorweed leaves, the beetles destroy some plants and make others so weak that other kinds of water plants can compete with it more successfully. (One of the competing plants is water hyacinth, another waterweed introduced from South America. Water hyacinths have become a problem in many areas, and researchers are seeking natural enemies to control this weed also.)

The stories of the Argentine ladybug, the prickly pear moth, and the insect enemies of the alligatorweed have

Insect fighters against alligatorweed: a moth, Vogtia malloi *(above) and the flea beetle* Agasicles hygrophila *(below).*

been success stories. But some insect invaders, which have come to other lands by invitation have quickly made their new hosts wish they had stayed at home.

One of the most serious threats to forests, shrubs, and gardens in the eastern United States today is the gypsy moth. The hairy, reddish-brown larvae of this moth can rapidly strip trees and bushes of every single leaf. When this happens, some trees die, and few trees can survive two or three straight years of gypsy-moth damage.

The hardy gypsy moth is not a native of the United States. In 1869, a naturalist named Leopold Trouvelot brought some gypsy moths over to Massachusetts from France. He hoped to cross these moths with silkworms and start a new textile industry. But instead, some of the moths escaped. Soon the woods of Massachusetts and neighboring states echoed with the noise of gypsy moth caterpillars' ceaseless chewing and the gentle rustle of falling, partly eaten leaves.

In 1953, federal and state authorities began a massive campaign to wipe out the gypsy moth by spraying infested areas with DDT. By 1958, they had nearly succeeded. But DDT was killing helpful insects and birds. And after a while there was so much DDT in soil and plants that cows began to pass the chemical along in their milk. DDT spraying was stopped, and Sevin, an insecticide that breaks down more quickly was substituted. But there were claims that this insecticide kills fish and fledgling birds, as well as bees and other helpful insects.

While people pick the caterpillars off trees and shrubs by hand and swat them with shovels, agricultural re-

A female gypsy moth lays her eggs on a twig (top); gypsy moth larvae on an oak leaf (middle); a gypsy moth trap (bottom).

searchers are working on more promising approaches. Germs that infect gypsy moths but leave other animals unharmed are being tried. The chemical scent that female gypsy moths send out to attract males has been isolated and made synthetically. Scientists have found that male gypsy moths are attracted to lures with the synthetic sex attractant. As a result they fly about confusedly, unable to find real female moths to mate with. Meanwhile, birds, beetles, and white-footed wood mice seem to be developing a taste for the gypsy moth caterpillars. Perhaps in time nature itself will bring this insect invader into balance.

What will the next insect invader be? Agricultural experts hope it will not be the khapra beetle. This devourer of grains and other stored foods has already spread from its native India to other parts of Asia, as well as to Europe and Africa. This beetle cannot fly, and thus it is spread from one country to another through shipping and trade. Agricultural inspectors have discovered khapra beetles in shipments of grains, as well as canned tuna, oil paintings, toys, imported cars, and crude rubber. Khapra beetles hide in burlap bags and wrapping materials. They can survive for years without food. In 1953, a khapra beetle infestation was discovered in California, Arizona, Texas, and New Mexico. The beetles were exterminated, but it cost more than $11 million to do it.

Agricultural inspectors at United States borders also keep a sharp watch for eggs and larvae of Mediterranean fruit flies in fruit shipments, and the eggs of the citrus blackfly on plant leaves. Meanwhile, agricultural experts are keeping a wary eye on the spread of another globe-hopping insect invader, now in South America: the African honeybee.

Honeybee raising is an important business in North and South America. In addition to making honey, the bees help to pollinate such crops as apples, citrus fruits, cotton, alfalfa, and cranberries. Farmers often do not depend on local bees to pollinate their crops. Instead they send to bee raisers for shipments of honeybees, which arrive just in time to do the job.

The honeybees raised in North and South America are not native to the Western Hemisphere. They are a variety of the European honeybee (*Apis mellifera ligustica*). These invited guests work hard to earn their keep. They spend their days out in the fields, flitting from flower to flower to gather nectar and pollen, which they bring back to their hive. Like ants, bees live in colonies of hundreds or thousands. There is a single queen in each hive, and a small number of males called drones, which do no work for the colony. All the tasks in the hive, from making wax honeycombs and turning nectar into honey, to caring for the queen and for the eggs she lays, are done by worker bees.

In 1956, a Brazilian scientist, Warwick Kerr, decided to try to improve the honeybee. He knew of another strain (*Apis mellifera adansonii*), which is native to Africa. The African honeybee is even harder working than its European cousin. African honeybees fly out to the fields earlier in the morning and work later at night. They can gather nectar on colder days than European honeybees can, and they even work through a light rain. As a result, they produce up to 80 percent more honey than European honeybees. Unfortunately these African wonderbees have one important fault: they have mean tempers. A European honeybee usually will not sting anyone unless she is attacked. But African honeybees sting without warning and without any provocation. And a person who is stung by an African honeybee is likely to be stung by more than one. All bees send out a sort of alarm chemical into the air when they sting, but scientists have found that African honeybees produce much more of this chemical than European honeybees do. When an African honeybee stings, all the other bees in the neighborhood become excited and swarm in for the attack.

Their short tempers make African honeybees difficult for beekeepers to handle, as well as a danger to people living in the area. They also have the annoying habit of swarming and leaving the hive suddenly, to make a new home somewhere else.

All these unpleasant traits should have been enough to make any sensible person leave African honeybees strictly alone. But Warwick Kerr had an idea. He thought he could crossbreed African honeybees with their gentler European relatives and come up with a sweet-tempered bee that would work just as hard as the nasty African bees.

Perhaps it would have worked. But before the Brazilian biologist had a chance to find out, someone accidentally left the screening off the cage with the African honeybees. Twenty-six African queen bees escaped and flew off into

African honeybees—hard-working pests.

the Brazilian countryside. There they promptly set up housekeeping and began to interbreed with the European honeybees that were there already. The breeding experiment was on in earnest!

Unfortunately, the new hybrid honeybees that began to spread out over South America were just as nasty as their African ancestors. They were strong and aggressive, and willing to nest almost anywhere. Often they drove out the milder-mannered European honeybees. Some beekeepers tried to raise the new bees. They were delighted with the bigger honey yields, and they gradually developed methods of working with the bees without getting stung. But the short-tempered bees stung people and animals all over the countryside, and a number of people died.

By the early 1970s, the African honeybees had spread

to Argentina, Uruguay, Paraguay, Bolivia, and parts of Peru, advancing at a rate of about 200 miles a year. Scientists had begun to fear that before they got the problem under control, people would be demanding that all bees be wiped out. Then what would happen to the crops that had to be pollinated?

Brazilian agriculturists have begun a program of raiding African honeybee hives to remove the queen and substitute a European honeybee queen, which has already mated. The African workers will care for her, but all the new bees that are born will be European honeybees. Other scientists are trying to breed a new and stronger honeybee that can compete with the African honeybee and keep it from spreading. The United States is helping in the research. For if this new insect invader is not defeated in South America, it is almost certain to spread to North America, too. And the African honeybee, for all its good qualities, is not wanted in the United States.

The Future of Animal Transplants

When we first moved to a home in the country, we were delighted with the wild neighbors we were seeing first-hand for the first time. In the woods and fields around our farm, we caught glimpses of cottontail rabbits, deer, squirrels, chipmunks, woodchucks, skunks, raccoons, weasels, birds of all shapes and colors, a black-and-white rabbit . . . a black-and-white rabbit? What on earth was a black-and-white rabbit doing running around loose in the fields of New Jersey? "Oh, that's Thumper," said our neighbor. "He used to be ours, but my son kept forgetting to feed him. I finally said, 'If you don't take care of that rabbit, I'm going to open his cage and turn him loose.' And the next time he forgot to feed the rabbit, that's exactly what I did."

As time went by, we discovered that many people in the area had turned pet rabbits loose, either accidentally or on purpose. We even inadvertently added to the wild rabbit population ourselves. That was before we knew that the European rabbit is a burrowing animal. We did not realize that you can't put a mother rabbit and her litter in a barn with a dirt floor and expect them to stay there. Once the little rabbits were loose, we didn't expect them to survive. They had been such trusting little creatures, raised in a peaceful environment where even the cats were not enemies. Yet winter has come and gone and we still see some of them hopping about. One recently had a litter in our chicken coop. (She would wait patiently in the morning for the door to be opened, so that she could go in and feed her babies.)

The United States government classes European rabbits among the harmful species, whose importation into the country is forbidden. Discussions of the rabbit invasion of Australia often go on to say, "If European rabbits should become established in the United States, . . ." We wonder when someone will notice that they already have. Yet it is not very likely that imported rabbits will become a serious pest in the United States. Unlike Australia and New Zealand, we have weasels, foxes, and numerous other predators quite capable of keeping rabbit populations in check. Even in areas where people have killed off the predators, there are various kinds of native rabbits and hares that would compete with the newcomers, and help to control their spread. Or at least we hope so.

It is not very likely that animal transplanting from country to country will stop. Insects and other pests will continue to slip through the borders as unsuspected hitchhikers. Imported pets will escape or be released by kind-hearted owners, and some will thrive and establish growing populations in new homes. And more and more, animals will be imported to try to readjust the balance of nature, to correct the mistakes of the past and the changes that our polluted age is making in the natural world.

The record of animal transplants so far has been sobering. For every brilliant success, there have been many cases in which the animal invader failed to become established, did not do what people hoped it would in its new home, or worse, became a serious pest. For the most part, it would seem to be safest not to meddle with the delicate balance of nature. Yet, as scientists learn more about how animals and plants interact with one another and with the world around them, there may be more animal transplants with happy results for all.

Australian scientists recently found a solution to one of their ecological problems in Africa. When settlers brought cattle and sheep to Australia, it was like a pebble dropping into the water and producing widening circles of ripples. Many of the effects of the importation were not realized at first. For example, it was a long time before anyone stopped to think that the Australian continent does not have any native dung beetles. Before there were cattle to leave their droppings on the plains, the absence of dung beetles did not matter. (Indeed, they would not have had anything to eat.) But the herds of cattle that live in Australia today deposit more than 33 million tons of dung each year. Bloodsucking pests called buffalo flies breed in the cattle droppings. The cattle dung covers the pasture land, and favors the growth of

Dung beetles play an important part in the balance of nature. (Above) a dung-burying beetle, Onthophagus bubalus; *(below) a dung ball rolling beetle,* Sisyphus rubripes. *Both were imported into Australia to solve a problem.*

patches of plants that cattle cannot eat. Without dung beetles to break up the dung and bury it in the soil, the cattle dung is no good as fertilizer. So Australian scientists searched through South Africa and found a number of beetles that could solve the problem. Some bury the dung, and others attack buffalo fly larvae in cattle dung. After tests to make sure that the beetles would not change their habits and become pests, hundreds of thousands of them were released and are now well established, working to restore the balance of nature.

Across the world, in California, scientists have been testing a tiny South American fish called the Argentine pearlfish, as a new approach to mosquito control. This tiny fish lays hundreds of eggs in the shallow waters of floodplains during the flooding season. When the floodwaters recede, the eggs remain in the drying mud. Some of them die, but many are preserved and hatch out the next year when the floods return. The tiny fish grow quickly, feeding on mosquito larvae. By the time the fish reach their full length of 2 or 3 inches, each one can eat up to fifty larvae a day. Researchers hope that these tiny fish can control mosquitoes in flooded rice fields and floodplains, especially in areas where the mosquitoes have become resistant to chemical insecticides.

Meanwhile, Israel is launched on a strange quest for foreign wildlife. Israeli wildlife biologists are trying to assemble a collection of the animals mentioned in the Bible that still remain on earth. The lion of Judah is extinct, and some of the other 120 Bible animals are close to extinction. Many of those that remain are no longer

Beasts of the Bible back in the Holy Land: the Somali ass (top left), ibex (top right), and a herd of addaxes (bottom).

to be found in the Holy Land. In 160 game preserves, Israel has now reestablished herds of gazelles and ibexes, as well as addaxes (a kind of antelope) and onagers (the ass that Jesus rode into Jerusalem). Somali wild asses, purchased in Ethiopia, and Arabian oryxes have joined the menagerie of this modern Noah's ark.

As man continues to change his world, how many countries of the future will have to venture abroad to reimport the animals that once were their own? And how many new animals will have to be brought in to control invaders with no natural enemies? No one can predict. The only thing that is certain is that the spread of living things from place to place is sure to continue with good results and bad.

Index

Achatina fulica (giant African snail), 84–91
addax, 119
Africa, imports from, 66, 68, 89, 109–110, 115–117
imports in, 29, 101, 108
Alaska, imports in, 68–69
amur, white, 81–83
ants, 44–45, 94–97 (*formica omnivora*), 44–45
red fire, 94–97
Apis mellifera adansonii (African honeybee), 109–112
Arizona, imports in, 108
Arkansas, imports in, 82–83
Asia, imports from, 17–18, 68, 74, 81, 108
imports in, 29, 89
ass, Somali wild, 119
Australia, imports from, 101
imports in, 29, 52–63, 101, 115–117

bats, fruit, 11
balance of nature, 10–11, 115
Barbados, imports to, 49
beetles, 26, 97–100, 101, 104, 108, 115–117
alligatorweed flea, 104
Australian ladybird, 101
dung, 115–117
elm bark, 97–100
Japanese, 26
khapra, 108
black buck, 68
blackfly, citrus, 108–109
Bufo marinus (giant toad), 45–46, 90–91

Cacto blastis cactorum (moth), 102
California, imports in, 6, 40, 101, 108, 117
carp
white amur, 81–83
catfishes, 11, 72–77
walking, 72–77
cattle, domestic
imported to Australia, 53, 115
China, imports from, 6–7
cichlids, 78, 80
clams, Chinese, 6–7
Clarias batrachus (walking catfish), 72–77
cockroaches, 92, 93
Columba livia (pigeon), 21–26
control of pest invaders, 9, 10, 24–26, 32, 37–38, 40–41, 42–50, 59–63, 70, 76–77, 80, 87–88, 90–91, 95–97, 97–100, 106–108, 114
ctenopharyngodon idella (white amur), 81–83
Cuba, imports from, 44
imports in, 49
damages done by invaders, 4–5, 8–9, 11, 24, 28, 31–32, 37, 40–41, 43–44, 49–50, 56, 59, 66, 68, 70, 76, 78, 86–88, 89, 90–91, 95–96, 97–98, 102, 110–111
competition with more valuable species, 8–9, 11, 28, 31–32, 66, 68, 76, 78, 90–91, 111
crop damage, 4–5, 9, 28, 31, 37, 40–41, 43–44, 49, 56, 59, 70, 108

diseases caused by, 24, 32,
49–50, 90, 97–98, 102
flooding, 41

deer, axis, 68
red, 70
Dendrosoter protuberans
(parasitic wasp), 98–100
dogs, in Australia, 53

East Coast of U.S.
imports in, 6
ecology, 11–12, 47
eland, 68
England, imports from, 26–29,
57–58, 70
imports in, 7–10, 39–40
Europe, imports from, 64, 93,
97, 106, 109, 113–114
imports in, 36–38, 39, 108
Equus caballus (mustang), 64–
66

flies, 93–94, 108
Hessian, 93–94
Mediterranean fruit, 108
Florida, imports in, 72–82

gazelle, 119
Georgia, imports in, 77
gnats, 93
good done by imports, 14–15,
82–83, 97, 100, 101, 102,
104, 109, 115–119
Greeks, ancient
pheasants, 16
use of pigeons, 21–22

Hawaii, imports from, 84
Herpestes javanicus (mongoose), 46–50
honeybee, African, 109–112

ibex, 66, 119
Siberian, 66
Israel, imports to, 117–119

Jamaica, imports in, 43–50

kudu, greater, 66

lizard, giant monitor, 90–91
Louisiana, imports in, 41

Massachusetts, imports in, 106
Mexico, imports from, 78
mice, 11, 53
mongooses, 11, 46–50
moth, 102, 106–108
gypsy, 106–108
muskrats, 34–38
mustangs, wild, 64–66
myiopsitta monachus (monk
parakeet), 3–6
Myocastor coypu (nutria), 38–
41
Myxomatosis, use of to control
rabbits, 61–63

New Jersey, imports in, 4
New Mexico, imports in, 66–68,
108
New York, imports in, 4, 27,
29–31
New Zealand, imports in, 29, 70
nilgai, 68
North America, imports from,
34–38
imports in, 39–41
see also United States, Mexico
nutria, 38–41

Ohio, imports in, 97
onager, 119
Ondatra zibethica (muskrat),
34–38
Oregon, imports in, 6, 18–19
Oryctolagus cuniculus (rabbit),
54–63
oryx, 68

parakeet, monk, 3–6
Passer domesticus (English
sparrow), 26

pearlfish, Argentina, 117
Pennsylvania, imports in, 4
pets, dealers and as invaders,
    3–4, 11–12, 72, 74–75, 84,
    88, 113
Phasianus colchicus (ring-
    necked pheasant), 13–20
pheasant, ring-necked, 13–20
pigeons, 21–26
pigs, Australia, 53
pike killifish, 78
piranha, 78–81
pollution and pesticides, 42–43
Porto Santo, rabbits on, 57
Puerto Rico, imports in, 49

rabbits, 53–63, 113–114
rats, 43–50, 53, 90, 91
    black, 43–50
    Norway, 43–50
reindeer, 68–69
Romans, 16–17, 56
    and pheasants, 16–17
    and rabbits, 56

Scolytus multistriatus (elm bark
    beetle), 97–100
Serrasalmus natterei (piranha),
    78–81
sheep, 53, 59, 66, 68, 115
    Barbary, 66
    mouflon, 68
Siberia, import from, 68

snail, giant African, 84–91
Solenopsis saevissima richteri
    (red fire ant), 94–97
South America, imports from,
    3–4, 6, 38–41, 79, 101, 104,
    117
    imports in, 29, 109–110
South Dakota, imports in, 19
sparrow, English, 21, 26–29
squirrel, gray, 7–10
starling, 21, 29–32
stem borer, alligatorweed, 104
Sturnus, vulgaris (starling), 29–
    32

Texas, imports in, 66, 67, 108
thrip, alligatorweed, 104
Tilapia, 80–81
toad, giant, 45–46, 90–91
transportation of imports, 3, 4,
    6–7, 10, 11, 12, 56–57, 72,
    84, 89–90, 92–94, 100–102,
    104, 108–109, 111, 114–115

United States, imports from,
    7–9
    imports in, 11–12, 17–19,
    64–66, 66–69, 71–83, 93–
    101, 103–108, 113–114, 117

wasp, parasitic, 98–100

zebra, 68

Credits

p. 5 (above) Courtesy Douglas Roscoe, N.Y. State Department,
Department of Environmental Conservation
(below) Courtesy J. Goerg
p. 8 Courtesy U.S. Department of the Interior
p. 15 Hal Harrison from Grant Heilman
p. 20 Leonard Lee Rue III from National Audubon Society
p. 23 Maurice E. Landre from National Audubon Society
p. 25 Maurice E. Landre from National Audubon Society
p. 27 Jeanne White from National Audubon Society
p. 30 (above) William J. Sahoda from National Audubon Society
(below) Eric J. Hosking from National Audubon Society
p. 37 (above) Grant Heilman
(below) Leonard Lee Rue from National Audubon Society
p. 40 Allan D. Cruickshank from National Audubon Society
p. 44 Courtesy U.S. Department of the Interior
p. 45 Dade Thornton from National Audubon Society
p. 48 (above) Mark Boulton from National Audubon Society
(below) Lewis Wayne Walker from National Audubon Society
p. 54 Courtesy Australian News and Information Bureau
p. 62 (above) Australian News and Information Bureau
(below) Courtesy Dr. Billie L. Padgett
p. 65 Courtesy Bureau of Sports Fisheries and Wildlife
p. 67 (top) Arthur Ambler from National Audubon Society
(bottom) Leonard Lee Rue from National Audubon Society
p. 69 Courtesy State of Alaska Department of Economic Development
p. 73 (top) Charles L. Trainer
(bottom) Courtesy Miami Seaquarium
p. 79 Arthur Ambler from National Audubon Society
p. 87 Courtesy Florida Department of Agriculture and Consumer Services
p. 94 Courtesy USDA
p. 96 (above) Courtesy Florida Department of Agriculture and
Consumer Affairs
(below) Courtesy USDA
p. 99 Courtesy USDA
p. 100 Courtesy USDA
p. 101 Courtesy USDA
p. 103 Courtesy USDA
p. 105 Courtesy USDA
p. 107 Courtesy USDA
p. 111 Courtesy José M. Ayres, University of São Paulo, Brazil
p. 116 Courtesy C.S.I.R.O. Division of Entomology

p. 118 (top left) Courtesy Holy Land Conservation Fund.
Photo by Benjamin Wechsler
(top right) Courtesy Holy Land Conservation Fund.
Photo by Micha Bar-Am
(bottom) Courtesy Holy Land Conservation Fund.
Photo by Itzhak Amit